PRAISE FOI

Keys to the Enneagram

"An inspiring, high-level offering from someone who deeply understands the process of spiritual realization for people who truly want to know how to use the Enneagram to liberate them from their ego and find the key to attaining a lived experience of eternal spirit."

—BEATRICE CHESTNUT, PHD
author of *The Complete Enneagram* and
The 9 Types of Leadership and coauthor of
The Enneagram Guide to Waking Up

"There are few teachers of consciousness, let alone Enneagram teachers, who can perceive, embody, articulate, and transmit the simultaneous arising of equal facets of spaciousness and singularity, expansion and particularity, personal love and emptiness, and personal will and surrender—all while focused on the vital need to awaken to our essential nature and potential. Like the Enneagram, A. H. Almaas himself is a tuning fork for this possibility of development and living. And somehow in *Keys to the Enneagram* he gently and firmly guides us onto that precise and expansive authentic path, beyond our fascination with personality. Before we know it, we have been initiated into a lineage of truth and Presence.

"I have had the honor of being the curator and host of the annual Enneagram Global Summit on the Shift Network since

2014 and have had meaningful, cutting-edge conversations with over a hundred Enneagram teachers. With absolute certainty, I can say that Almaas is among a very few teachers whose constant aim is to awaken themselves and be in service to others' awakening. He *never* approaches the Enneagram with the slightest bit of derision toward, or reification of, personality, and he is unparalleled in this in my experience. His compass never wavers from its direction home—to real self and to reality—that, by the way, supports the emergence of each individual's true purpose and offering to this life.

"This book is perhaps the first to so keenly and clearly articulate a growing realization among some of us who teach the Enneagram for awakening that the transformational power of working with all nine fixations and journeying on all nine paths of essential qualities is paramount. If you want to awaken to your true self and follow a North Star to wholeness and liberation through compassion and learning from your ego, pick up and read *Keys to the Enneagram*. You will have a North Star in your very own hands and eyes."

—JESSICA DIBB
founder and director of Inspiration Consciousness
School and founder and host of the Shift Network
Annual Enneagram Global Summit

Keys to the
ENNEAGRAM

*How to Unlock the Highest Potential
of Every Personality Type*

A. H. ALMAAS

With a foreword by
Russ Hudson

and an afterword by
Sandra Maitri

SHAMBHALA

Shambhala Publications, Inc.
2129 13th Street
Boulder, Colorado 80302
www.shambhala.com

Excerpts from *Ennea-type Structures: Self-Analysis for the Seeker* by Dr. Claudio Naranjo (Gateways Books & Tapes, 1991) included by permission of the publisher.

Excerpts from *The Wisdom of the Enneagram: The Complete Guide to Psychological and Spiritual Growth for the Nine Personality Types* by Don Richard Riso and Russ Hudson, copyright © 1999 by Don Riso and Russ Hudson. Used by permission of Bantam Books, an imprint of Random House, a division of Penguin Random House LLC. All rights reserved.

Excerpts from *The Spiritual Dimension of the Enneagram: Nine Faces of the Soul* by Sandra Maitri (Jeremy Tarcher/Putnam, 2000) included by permission of the author.

Cover art: robin.ph/Shutterstock, KatMoy/Shutterstock, VerisStudio/Shutterstock, Tiffy Studio/Shutterstock
Cover design: Shubhani Sarkar
Interior design: Kate Huber-Parker

9 8 7 6 5 4 3 2

Printed in the United States of America

♾ This edition is printed on acid-free paper that meets the American National Standards Institute Z39.48 Standard.
♻ This book is printed on 30% postconsumer recycled paper.
For more information please visit www.shambhala.com.

Shambhala Publications is distributed worldwide by Penguin Random House, Inc., and its subsidiaries.

Library of Congress Cataloging-in-Publication Data
Names: Almaas, A. H., author. | Hudson, Russ, writer of foreword. | Maitri, Sandra, 1949– writer of afterword.
Title: Keys to the enneagram: how to unlock the highest potential of every personality type / A. H. Almaas; with a foreword by Russ Hudson and an afterword by Sandra Maistri.
Description: First edition. | Boulder, Colorado: Shambhala, [2021] | Includes bibliographical references and index.
Identifiers: LCCN 2020053742 | ISBN 9781611809435 (trade paperback)
Subjects: LCSH: Enneagram.
Classification: LCC BF698.35.E54 A46 2021 | DDC 155.2/6—dc23
LC record available at https://lccn.loc.gov/2020053742

Dedicated to

THE SARMOUN DARQ—

the original source of the Enneagram,
the ancient spiritual school whose grace and intention
are an important current in the Diamond Approach.

CONTENTS

FOREWORD

At the time of this writing, something very unexpected is occurring. The Enneagram, part of an ancient teaching on the inner development of human beings, has emerged from the shadows of relative obscurity and is exploding into wide-ranging public attention. Once known only in certain specific spiritual schools, it has become almost mainstream. Popular articles in magazines and on the internet have proliferated to such a degree that people with the slightest interest in psychology or spirituality are likely to have heard of it. New publications on the subject arrive with greater and greater frequency and dozens of people are presenting themselves as teachers and guides in the growing Enneagram marketplace. From one point of view, this is encouraging and may reflect a genuine desire for self-knowledge in the midst of a society presented with a plethora of confusing and sometimes contradictory messages about who we are and what life is truly about. But this newfound popularity also comes at a price.

The basics of the Enneagram are fairly easy to grasp, which may account for some of its rapid growth. We learn that this system describes nine types of people and after learning about each type, we do some self-reflection and decide which one fits us best. People often report amazement at how well the Enneagram can describe not only our outer behaviors but also some of our inner motivations. It can be startling to feel so understood. We then might move on to deducing the types of family members, friends, and loved ones, not to mention celebrities or historic figures we admire. We feel like we have received an amazing new lens for seeing people more accurately. But as we dig a little deeper, we may discover that the system is more complex than we originally realized. We find that there are many different aspects to the Enneagram, not to mention many diverse theories. We may experience great excitement in sharing the latest theories with fellow Enneagram enthusiasts, but we may also feel confused by the sometimes conflicting perspectives on the system now available in the marketplace. We might wonder if there is something more to it than this.

If we persist in our explorations, we eventually realize that while there are many intriguing descriptions of the nine types and their variations, knowing these descriptions does not necessarily lead to any real change or development. At this point, some become frustrated with the Enneagram and move on to other interests, while others remain satisfied to continue discussing theories about the types. Some even learn to use the knowledge they have gathered to *avoid* being affected by any deeper realizations about themselves. It becomes easier to look like an "expert" on the subject than to continue into the territories of real self-knowledge and the feelings such knowledge can bring up. But some of us cannot resist the deepening mystery, and we start to consider more of what is available through this work.

A bigger truth may then strike us. The Enneagram, in its original sense, was never meant to be a "filing system" for human beings. We can indeed see that there is something true and helpful about recognizing the patterns of type, but it is important to remember that these type patterns *do not reflect our true identity*. It would be more accurate to say that awareness of the type patterns can potentially awaken us to the more profound realizations of who or what we are beyond all of these patterns. But this cannot happen simply by intellectually studying the types or by endlessly telling ourselves and others stories about being our type. Discussions of our type can be useful, but they are meant to be in service to a more central process—what is traditionally called *inner work*. To understand what that means, it may be helpful to look at some of the background of this system.

If we explore the roots of the Enneagram, we will not find a clear, single history behind it. Rather, we will see that related teachings connected with it have appeared and become interwoven with each other in different ways throughout history right back into the preclassical civilizations of the ancient world. We start to see that beyond type descriptions, the Enneagram is part of a vast philosophical framework that looks at the nature of the human psyche and its place in a larger cosmos. There are elements of the Enneagram that arise out of the teachings of ancient Egypt and Mesopotamia. These find their way into the mystical expressions of the three prophetic religions of the West: Judaism, Christianity, and Islam. Other elements appear most vividly in the rise of Greek philosophy, going back to pre-Socratics like Pythagoras, and through Socrates to Plato and the Neoplatonist schools that thrived during the Roman Empire. Elements continue in the Hermetic traditions in the Middle Ages and Renaissance as well as in the mysteries of the Jewish Kabbalah, some of the northern schools of Sufism, and in the monastic traditions of contemplative Christianity.

You may notice that while these teachings were part of the well-established religious and philosophical traditions of Western civilization, they were not mainstream. Various aspects of the teachings were cultivated and preserved in spiritual schools and generally only known within them. But central to all these teachings was *the necessity of practice.* These teachings were not intellectual speculations but were the fruit of people earnestly engaged in spiritual practices for long periods of time. In other words, the Enneagram teachings about the types were meant to accompany psychological and spiritual practices for the development of consciousness. And central to these traditions was the necessity of cultivating *presence*—which is really at the core of most mystical teachings. For me, the Enneagram without the focus on presence is not really the Enneagram.

To truly grasp the range of what we will be learning in this book, we need to recognize that authentic modern Enneagram work has three main elements: the symbol, the typology, and the system of practice behind it. The more we are aware of these three components, the more fruitful our work with the Enneagram will be.

The symbol was originally brought to the attention of the modern world by the great spiritual teacher George Gurdjieff. He began teaching it to students in Russia at the beginning of the twentieth century and later to students in France, the United Kingdom, and the United States. While Gurdjieff taught a great deal about the symbol and its meanings, he did not use the symbol in conjunction with a system of nine types. If he knew of such correlations, he declined to teach them to any of his students. He taught the Enneagram as a mandala showing certain key elements of human consciousness. Understanding the symbol was a way of opening our dualistic thinking to a mode of perceiving reality in more of its dynamic wholeness. He described the three components of the symbol—the circle, the triangle, and the hexad shape—as the bases of three fundamental laws of consciousness: The Law of One, the Law of Three, and the Law of Seven. In short, the Law of One reminds us of the oneness or unity of existence. The Law of Three looks at how discrete phenomena arise and return to the fundamental ground of unity. And the Law of Seven looks at how anything manifested within the unity undergoes constant change and process according to universal laws. When you put these perspectives together, you can see that Gurdjieff used the symbol to approach teachings of nonduality in a way that preserved the sense of the underlying unity of reality in relation to the diverse, ever-changing phenomena we can perceive through our senses.

He also taught the symbol as a map of any complete process and as a way of comprehending the complex interactions within all real and living systems. So while Gurdjieff did not teach the nine types, he did bring many of the teachings associated with Enneagram work to the fore, including the concept of essence and personality, which is the notion that in our ordinary state we are asleep to ourselves and to greater reality; and the concept of the centers of intelligence—the instinctual intelligence of the body, the emotional intelligence of the heart, and the cognitive intelligence of the head—which are pivotal in learning how we can actually use this knowledge for our maturation and development. It would be fair to say that much of the philosophical framework behind the Enneagram was presented by Gurdjieff.

Gurdjieff considered the Enneagram to be part of a larger corpus of teachings he called the Fourth Way and would certainly have held the view that the symbol would be of limited use to someone not aware of the overall orientation of the Fourth Way. The notion of this approach to awakening is based on the idea of working with the centers of intelligence. Gurdjieff taught that each primary path to liberation depended on working with one of these centers. The First Way has to do with mastering the instincts of the body. The Second Way is about transforming the emotions into the deeper, more essential qualities of the heart. The Third Way is about mastering our busy, constantly churning thoughts and opening to the pristine stillness and silence of deeper mind. Gurdjieff also taught that all three of these paths had been available throughout history for the serious seeker of the divine, but that all were in some sense renunciate paths, requiring us to forego most, if not all, of our usual worldly concerns. They involved solitude or monastic life. Yet he held that there was a Fourth Way that required a much more developed knowledge and system of practice because it entailed working on *all three centers at once*—the body, heart, and mind. Further, the Fourth Way was to be a way of life—not a monastic path, yet taken on with the same devotion and dedication as one would assume in entering a monastery. Lastly, he emphasized that the Fourth Way was not always available. That it appeared in certain stages of history as a kind of "help" provided when humanity was at a major crossroads—what he called a "shock point"—and that we were at such a crossroads in our time. It might be said that while information about the Enneagram can be used in any number of ways, its core and original purpose was as a part of the larger purposes and orientation of the Fourth Way. Teachers who know this carry a certain "flavor." They are transmitting something beyond the information about the Enneagram types.

The typology associated with the Enneagram was presented to the world by the Bolivian teacher and founder of the Arica School, Oscar Ichazo. Like Gurdjieff, Ichazo used the Enneagram as a way of framing work for students engaged in long-term spiritual practice and within the structures of a spiritual school. He brought many brilliant and masterful insights into the corpus of teachings connected with the symbol, and it would be entirely reasonable to say that the modern Enneagram movement would not exist without him.

One of Ichazo's greatest contributions was mapping several related schemas of the soul drawn from the great spiritual traditions of the world onto the Enneagram symbol. This was no small feat. Not only did he draw on a profound understanding of these other maps, but he was able to place their elements in the correct sequence around the nine points of the symbol, perhaps taking to heart Gurdjieff's suggestion that we would truly see new vistas of any set of phenomena if we could accurately place them on the symbol. He drew on teachings from esoteric Buddhism, Taoism, and other Eastern traditions but more centrally from Western esoteric teachings—principally from Kabbalah, the monastic traditions of the Christian Desert Fathers, the Neoplatonic teachings on the soul from Plotinus and others, and some of the practices and methods of transmission from the heart of Sufism.

Ichazo was interested in much more than a description of personality types, and he mapped many elements of nature and human consciousness on the Enneagram, although he called the symbol an Enneagon. He created 108 Enneagons in all, each revealing particular teachings about the self and reality. The modern Enneagram movement is based almost entirely on four of these Enneagons: the Enneagon of the passions, the Enneagon of the virtues, the Enneagon of the fixations, and the Enneagon of the holy ideas. I would add that through much of the Enneagram field, the virtues and the holy ideas are not included, even though from the Fourth Way perspective, they are the point of learning the system.

Much of the basis of the Enneagon of the passions was drawn from the first monastic communities in the Christian world—the

Desert Fathers of Egypt. This is significant because their work provides us with a clue about the original sense and purpose of the type material. Much of what we know about the practices of these first Christian monastics is the result of Evagrius of Pontus, an early Christian theologian who described the prayers and meditations the monks were engaging in and their discovery of eight "sins" that they grappled with in their efforts to develop and sustain their inner connection with God. These sins were not seen as evil activities but as the distractions from their practices—as ways they lost presence and the direct awareness of the divine reality within them and around them. Over time, the monks provided various names for these ways of "missing the mark." The historical record includes some variations on these names, but they were most commonly called anger or wrath, pride, vanity or vainglory, envy, avarice, gluttony, lust, and sloth—also known as acedia or sadness. Evagrius also broadly described a ninth problematic condition, and it was further discussed and described by later theologians including Pseudo-Dionysius the Areopagite. It came to be called doubt or faithlessness. As you may notice, some of these vexations went on to become the seven deadly sins in Christianity, although there were originally eight or nine of them.

We can then appreciate that Ichazo mapped some of the characteristics of higher consciousness onto the nine points of the Enneagram symbol and also, inspired by the work of the Desert Fathers and Mothers, mapped the corresponding psychological conditions created by the loss of contact with these more direct experiences of presence resulting in the Enneagons of the passions (the deadly sins) and the fixations (the arrested and limited view of reality that ego creates). Thus, each point was not a final statement about a person but an indication of a particular way of forgetting presence, and thus, forgetting our true nature—our true identity. How Ichazo managed to accomplish this amazing feat was probably a combination of dedicated scholarship and profound intuition. There were precedents in spiritual teachings that likely provided him with clues. In medieval Christianity, theologians who had been exposed to Evagrius's ideas about the sins sought to determine a correct order for them, and even Pope Gregory I came close to describing the sequence we find in the Enneagram. It is likely that Ichazo also got insights from certain patterns within the tree of life in the Kabbalah—a source he often cited as a major inspiration. The end result of this effort was the correct placement of the nine type energies around the Enneagram symbol.

To some extent, the typology and the symbol can be understood intellectually, and in some parts of the Enneagram community, things stop right there. But the third element, the system of practice behind it, is another matter. In my view, the Enneagram does not really come to life to assist us in our development without this vital third component. And it is here that the importance of A. H. Almaas, and the work he describes in this book, becomes most central and evident.

I originally learned about the Enneagram through the Gurdjieff Work, and I was fortunate to study with some of the great teachers who had worked directly with Gurdjieff during his life. When I encountered the first books on the Enneagram typology in the late 1980s, I had already been steeped in the inner spiritual practices of the Gurdjieff Work for many years but had become convinced that additional insights into the core of human nature might be useful. And since the Enneagram of personality clearly had some connection to what I had been studying, it made sense to investigate it. Reading those early books on the Enneagram typology, I was impressed by the detail with which some of the early authors approached the descriptions of the nine types. This seemed to me helpful information, and I could see how these insights could be an enormous support to someone engaged in inner work. Yet none of the books I encountered seemed to know much about the real roots and purpose of the material, let alone the meaning of the symbol itself.

As it turned out, I lived a short distance from one of the major Enneagram authors, Don Richard Riso, who had written the seminal book *Personality Types*. I read his book and sought him out for a consultation about my Enneagram type. That conversation evolved into a friendship and ultimately into a teaching and writing team. Don Riso had received his initial training with the Jesuits and had worked on his book for some twelve years, yet he was well aware that there was much more to the system than what he had learned. I introduced him to the Gurdjieff Work, and together we sought to reunite the fascinating typology with the orientation of Fourth Way inner work described by Gurdjieff. Particularly, we sensed that there had to be a way that each of the nine Enneagram points, beyond being a type of person, also reflected a particular journey from identification with the ego or personality to a realization of the self as essence. This was the whole point of such studies from a Fourth Way point of view.

As we engaged in our studies and the practices of the Gurdjieff Work, we also became more aware of the writings of A. H. Almaas, and particularly his first major book, *Essence*. It seemed to us that Almaas had already been exploring the challenge we had taken on, and we were profoundly impressed and impacted by the clarity of his writing, his thought, and his approach. We saw that he had seen deeply into the relationship between egoic consciousness and the amazing and profound worlds of essence.

We learned that he had created a spiritual school called Ridhwan (also called the Diamond Approach), and that he had developed practices for exploring the patterns of the psyche and opening up awareness of our true nature, our essence. As our tenure in the Gurdjieff Work came to an end, we sought out Almaas's teachings and joined a Diamond Approach group, and this became our spiritual home for the years that followed.

As I became more familiar with Almaas and his work, I learned that he had acquired knowledge of the Enneagram typology from the Chilean psychiatrist Claudio Naranjo. Naranjo was the first to bring Oscar Ichazo's teachings on the nine points as passions and fixations to the United States in the early 1970s. In California and other places, Naranjo formed a group to study various systems of realization and to work with the Enneagram typology. The group was called SAT (Seekers after Truth) and Almaas was an original member of that group. While part of that group, he began to have a series of inner experiences and realizations that led to the development of the Diamond Approach. And as it was with Gurdjieff's teachings and Ichazo's Arica School, the Enneagram became just a part of the much larger body of teachings of the Diamond Approach.

When I began attending meetings and retreats of the Diamond Approach, I noticed that Almaas and the school in general had the distinct flavor of a Fourth Way teaching. In that sense, it felt in great alignment with what I had already been studying and with what most awakened my heart. At the same time, some of the practices were distinctly different from what we had done in the Gurdjieff Work. At the center of these practices was the orientation of *inquiry*, which for me was a Fourth Way approach of bringing the full intelligence of the centers to whatever phenomenon was arising in our consciousness. It entails grounded presence, openheartedness, and a willingness to experience with an open, receptive quality of mind. We learn not to reject our experience, and when we can bring the fullness of presence to anything arising in us, consciousness itself, or Grace, if you will, transforms the experience into something more profound and helpful. Like all inner practices, it takes a while to get the sense of inquiry. But I soon realized and appreciated what Almaas had discovered: that bringing this inquiring awareness to the patterns of personality described in the Enneagram typology could open us up quickly and powerfully to new experiences of what we actually are.

One of the most profound realizations that Almaas shared with us, and that he describes elegantly in this book, is that essence manifests in different qualities—one might even say different tastes, colors, and textures. Some esoteric literature I had explored in the traditions of Sufism and Tantric Buddhism touched on this topic, but Almaas had found ways to make this teaching explicit and central in his approach to inner work. And more importantly, he had been exploring and mapping the relationship between various psychological states, defenses, and barriers with the perceived loss of the direct experience of specific essential qualities. In other words, he had been developing the very idea explored by the Desert Fathers but was seeing into the *cause* of these psychological patterns. This was profound knowledge about the core inner relationship upon which I had become convinced the Enneagram types were formed. This was an earthshaking discovery. I suspect over time, spiritual seekers around the world will come to understand how helpful and powerful this perspective on human nature can be.

In *Keys to the Enneagram*, Almaas delivers on the title of the book. He elucidates the specific inner relationships between core essential states of the soul, their perceived loss in childhood, and the psychological defenses and difficulties that arise to cover over the apparent loss of essential qualities. These patterns are specific and really do constitute the core of any real Enneagram work. Of course, the more you acquire a dedicated practice to cultivate presence and the capacity to observe the activities of your inner world, the more this book will come to life and be a tremendous friend to you on your journey. I feel these teachings are an enormous gift to anyone engaged in the process of awakening, regardless of your path or faith orientation.

In 1999, Almaas wrote an Enneagram book called *Facets of Unity*, and it remains the foundational text for the teachings of the holy ideas—advanced material on the various nondual perceptions of reality that arise when the mind is liberated from each point's characteristic fixation. This is a hugely important book for advanced students, but Almaas saw that for many of the students of the Enneagram, a more introductory approach to using the Diamond Approach in conjunction with the Enneagram was required, and thus this book came into being. If you sincerely work with the practices and ideas in this book, you will develop a deeper understanding of yourself and of the topics in *Facets of Unity*.

I have been a student of Almaas and the Diamond Approach school now for many years. Having a community of sincere seekers to study with has truly supported my work with my students, and I can say that even after decades of studying with Almaas, he still surprises me on a regular basis with amazing new insights into the human condition. He and his teaching partner, Karen Johnson, have continued to provide a framework for profoundly life-changing teachings and practices, and the school has in many ways been the backbone of my own spiritual journey. Yet until now, Almaas has kept much of his approach to the Enneagram within the Ridhwan School. You hold in your hands some of his wisdom on this topic, distilled through many years of practice and experience.

I feel that this book is part of the genuine transmission that is the source of the Enneagram teachings. It has the flavor, the feeling, of real Fourth Way teaching, and I suspect that reading it with a sincere heart and working with the ideas you will find in it, may put you in touch with that source. Almaas, known to us also as Hameed Ali, reveals openly this source in the first pages of the book. I find this a fitting invitation for you, the reader, and a reminder that the shock point for humanity that Gurdjieff spoke of is here. May we all receive whatever we need to respond to the inner wisdom seeking to arise in our hearts. Great gratitude to A. H. Almaas for this huge contribution to the Enneagram work.

RUSS HUDSON
New York City
October 14, 2020

EDITOR'S PREFACE

Keys to the Enneagram is a new contribution to the growing body of knowledge about the Enneagram and its nine personality types. Much has been written about the psychological understanding contained in this ancient conceptualization of the human psyche. This book expands on this wisdom by offering a unique perspective to those exploring, studying, and teaching the Enneagram. In the pages that follow, Almaas reveals the spiritual qualities linked to each Enneatype. Exploring how these qualities inform and transform the fixations can be a powerful tool for spiritual awakening.

This book is a companion volume to *Facets of Unity*, a book published by Almaas in 1998. The latter book describes the spiritual foundation of the Enneagram of personality by articulating the Enneagram of holy ideas. These are the nine enlightened perspectives on reality that correspond with the nine Enneatypes. The root of each Enneatype is its disconnection from Being and simultaneously from its holy idea. As a result, each Enneatype develops a delusional perspective on reality that leads to the fixation of the personality. *Facets of Unity* provides a detailed understanding of how this fundamental disconnection happens and the resulting distorted perspective of the fixated Enneatype.

Keys to the Enneagram looks at a different dimension of the Enneagram of personality. As we know, each Enneatype takes on certain strategies and behaviors based on its distorted view of reality. Through the lens presented in *Keys* we see that these manifestations are shaped by a belief that there is an ideal way to function and appear. This is referred to as the ego ideal. The holy idea is the deeper perspective of truth that is lost when the Enneatype becomes disconnected from its deeper ground. The ego ideal is a vision of optimal functioning that the Enneatype orients toward to compensate for this disconnection. What *Keys* does is elucidate the spiritual qualities that the nine ego ideals are unconsciously mimicking. These qualities are actual states of being that shape and color our individual consciousness from the inside. If recognized and embodied, they will relax the fixated orientation of the Enneatype and open the way for recovering the perspective of the spiritual ground of reality.

There is a fundamental principle of the Diamond Approach path that Almaas is drawing on in sharing his understanding of these keys to the Enneagram. This is the recognition that the ego self is not fundamentally original; it cannot develop original solutions for life's problems. Only Being itself—the living existence of consciousness—can respond to reality in creative and original ways. Ego's responses to life are a product of its ideas and learning—concepts, beliefs, plans, judgments, and conditioning from the past. Since ego lacks beingness—direct immediate existence—it can only construct responses from what it has already known. This means it cannot create anything new or fresh. It must copy or restructure something from the past. All of its forms and responses to life are some effort to mimic or simulate what Being has originally manifested. Thus ego gets all of its ideas, all of its strategies, all of its possibilities from Being, usually without knowing it.

It is this principle that is at the heart of *Keys to the Enneagram*. Each Enneatype is built around an ego ideal. But this ideal is not something that is a result of choice or conditioning; it is not a product of upbringing. This ideal came about as a reflection of something real, a way that Being actually manifests that is no longer accessible. Though the ego ideal exists now as a mental concept of ideal behavior or functioning, it arose as an unconscious effort to recapture a particular state of being, a flavor of living consciousness. In the Diamond Approach these states are known as essential aspects or qualities. And each one is characterized by a sense of presence, of direct felt immediacy and hereness that is not mental.

This understanding is one of the central realizations that the spiritual path of the Diamond Approach offers to those engaged in inner work. All the ego manifestations we develop as we grow up—the various ways we attempt to control our experience, defend our vulnerability, and compensate for our deficiencies—are actually distorted and hollow approximations of the spiritual capacities and qualities we were all born with but have lost touch with through our upbringing, our family conditioning. This is a very helpful and hopeful recognition as it awakens us to the inherent intelligence in our soul. We can feel nourished by the fact that something in us knows our deeper nature and wants to recover it—even if we are going about it in an indirect, ignorant, and ineffective way. And we can contact and be held by that deeper ground if we are willing to be curious and explore the undercurrents in our personal experience.

In *Keys to the Enneagram*, Almaas is inviting us to undertake this journey by beginning with the familiar nine fixations of the Enneagram, the world of personality types. Rather than simply type ourselves and those around us and then analyze behaviors and patterns, he asks us to look deeper. What is really going on here? Why relate to a particular ego ideal? Why are they important?

The ego ideals that govern each of the nine points can open us up to our spiritual nature and its many qualities if we are willing to take a deeper look. This book will support that personal inquiry. I believe you will find that Almaas's words provide guidance and inspiration for understanding yourself more deeply as you awaken to your spiritual nature.

BYRON BROWN
Editor

ACKNOWLEDGMENTS

I would like to thank Jorge Arango for his attentive and careful editing of my original manuscript for this book. He brought his knowledge of the Enneagram to the challenging task of shaping my words into an effective book for the reader. He collaborated in this process with my chief editor, Byron Brown, whose many years of involvement with my books helped guide this material into a final form that you have in your hands. I feel gratitude to both Jorge and Byron for their work together on this book.

My thanks to Alexis St. John for creating the Enneagram diagrams in Appendix 3.

In addition, I feel indebted to Liz Shaw, my editor at Shambhala Publications, for her supportive and clear-eyed feedback in pointing out places that needed further attention. Over many years of working together, she has come to know my work and appreciate the ways it can be most accessible and useful for a growing audience.

I would also like to express my appreciation to Sandra Maitri and Russ Hudson for being willing to contribute to this effort of bringing elements of essential understanding to the study of the personality fixations of the Enneagram.

Keys to the
ENNEAGRAM

INTRODUCTION

The knowledge of the Enneagram in the West started with G. I. Gurdjieff, who said that during his trip to the Hindu Kush, he received his understanding from the Sarmoun brotherhood—a mysterious mystical school whose existence he dated to 2500 BCE. After him came Oscar Ichazo, who said his source for the Enneatypes (Enneagram of types) was the Sarmoun and/or Sufi sources. Through visionary insights, Ichazo developed this initial knowledge to describe many levels of the Enneagram, applying them to different domains of human experience. This immense body of knowledge became important for the spiritual teaching he gave to the Arica School, making up its central organizing element.

While studying with Ichazo in Bolivia, Dr. Claudio Naranjo received the knowledge of the Enneagram and filled it out with his extensive psychological learning, especially traits (or dispositional) theory. From him it passed to some of his students and beyond. The Enneagram field has by now been applied to countless human activities and interests and has been written about extensively. This makes sense, for the original teaching was presented as a map of reality that can clarify any area of life or study. The Enneagram community has become a worldwide network of writers, teachers, and seekers who find it useful for their life, work, or inner spiritual maturation.

I was a member of Naranjo's first SAT (Seekers after Truth) group, and I learned many of the levels of the Enneagram from him. The Enneagram is fundamentally a dynamic flow that connects nine points around a circle by a nonlinear path. Gurdjieff was one of the first to use this flow as it applied to many areas of experience in the human (and natural) world. Ichazo focused on it as a tool of human study. Naranjo used it as a psychological tool to investigate the ego personality that keeps our essential/spiritual nature hidden or inaccessible. Based on his work and that of other followers of Ichazo, the Enneagram has become known almost exclusively for its application to patterns in human psychology and spiritual development. In this context, the nine points have become more of the focus, and the flow between them is less understood and often forgotten.

Naranjo was also a student of Karen Horney, from whom he learned self-analysis, an approach he imparted to his students. As a result, we spent several years deeply immersed in this self-study. For everyone in the group it was an intense time as we were learning about the workings of our psychological makeup. Even as we did a great deal of psychological processing, our orientation was always spiritual, supported by ongoing meditation practices.

We mostly studied the Enneagram of fixations, with some reference to the Enneagrams of passions and virtues, holy ideas, and instincts. The fixations refer to nine personality types where the perspectives and characteristics of each have become fixated patterns in the average human psyche. The passions are the nine ways the emotional heart energy of human beings gets stuck; the virtues are the nine spiritual attitudes that counteract the passions. The holy ideas are nine spiritually enlightened perspectives on reality that underlie the personality fixations, while becoming distorted and obscured by those fixated patterns. And the instincts are nine ways that the three basic instincts (survival, sexual, and social) appear in the nine fixations.

Toward the end of that time in 1973, we were given a practice called the "three days of prayer," which was done in solitude. I prayed constantly for hours at a time each day. On the third day, after the prayers had exposed the pretenses of ego, I had a profound and complete experience of ego death. But it was not just an ego death experience, or awakening, as the term is used these days. It was a particular kind of ego death, which I refer to as the Sarmoun-type of ego death, to differentiate it from other types of ego death that occurred at later times. As I saw the pretenses and identifications of ego clearly, I felt quite helpless to break free of them, for they happened so fast, one after the other, like an unstoppable stream of impressions, thoughts, and beliefs. At this point—when I saw there was nothing I could do to free myself because I was too mired in ego—there occurred a descent of spiritual grace or energy. I felt myself showered with, immersed in, and enveloped by a fluid substance of pure consciousness. It felt rich and viscous and tasted sweet—like a dense golden honey of spiritual abundance, transparent and divinely ecstatic. Only later, as the Diamond Approach was developing in the late seventies and afterward, did I recognize that the sweet fullness pervading my consciousness was a kind of presence. It was the presence of consciousness, or spiritual nature, in the quality of honey, a quality that reveals the abundance and richness of true nature in the most explicit and definitive way.

But this abundance was not just an experience of the divine honey. It was a force that penetrated and impacted the whole of my body, mind, and consciousness so thoroughly that none of them remained. As I was being deliciously overwhelmed by this wonderful ecstatic love, I could hear the sound of bees all around me. I melted in honey, in the midst of the gentle and relaxing buzzing of what seemed to be thousands of bees. Of course, there were no bees in the room. This interior sound is associated with the aspect of honey. I refer to this ego death as the Sarmoun type because one meaning of Sarmoun Darq is "community of bees," and its work is to collect spiritual nectars and wisdom and preserve them for when humanity needs them. The Sarmoun members are like the bees who collect the honey of our precious nature and preserve it for times when spiritual teachings require renewal and an infusion of spiritual grace.

I call this phenomenon ego death because it literally was a ceasing of ego. The honey so overwhelmed and penetrated my consciousness that it completely melted it. But it did so in love and ecstasy. It melted everything all the way to total annihilation of conscious experience. I was no more, there was no me, not even the knowing of "no me." It was a total cessation of individual consciousness, to the point of no experience at all. Loving presence was so strong and dominant that no fear or trepidation manifested, nor any resistance or hesitation. I don't know how long I stayed in this divine coma, but when I awoke, everything was crystal clear, and there was realization that enlightenment had happened. It did not last, for there were many things that still needed to be worked out. That working out happened in the following years through the development of the Diamond Approach, which brought many more ego deaths and many other awakenings.

The salient point here is not that I had an ego death experience, or what is called total cessation of all perception and sensation. What turned out to be important and lasting is that it was specifically a death into honey amid the buzzing of bees. It was a Sarmoun death that marked a deep connection with the Sarmoun and their current of blessings, style of teaching, and spiritual mission. This became an underlying current in the development of the Diamond Approach, opening the way to a lasting connection with the Sarmoun consciousness and mission. My insights into the Enneagram are only part of this connection.

I believe it is this connection, in addition to many types of revelation in the Diamond Approach, that made it possible for me to receive the inspired understanding of the holy ideas. That happened in the early nineties, and the understanding became part of the canon of the Diamond Approach teaching. I wrote about part of that knowledge of the holy ideas in my book *Facets of Unity*, which offers an experiential appreciation of the holy ideas as facets of mature and complete nondual realization. It also explains what leads to the loss of access to this understanding and what results due to this loss: the formation of the core of each fixation.

The fixation of each type, I discovered, is constituted by a core and a shell. The two are connected but based on two different levels of spiritual experience. My focus then was on the core. I did not think of writing at the time about how the shell forms and what the principles of its formation are. Sandra Maitri, in her book *The Spiritual Dimension of the Enneagram*, included this understanding as part of her detailed exposition of the Enneagram.

It has been twenty years since *Facets of Unity* was published. Only recently have I realized that I have more understanding to share about the Enneagram, which has led to the creation of this book as a companion to the first. I have been feeling the necessity to complete that work, specifically to write about the fixation shells, for in these shells lie the secret keys that we need to unlock each fixation and tackle the difficult and deep task of working through the inner cores. I use the word *key* to refer to an essential aspect or quality that reveals the inner logic of each fixation, while also providing a means to "unfix" it. I am not going to be discussing the details of each type and its fixation. Many authors, including Sandra Maitri, Claudio Naranjo, Helen Palmer, and Russ Hudson, have done a great job in spelling these out. Rather, I will use the knowledge of the Enneagram to find the key to each type that is necessary to gain freedom from the fixation.

In my experience, it is quite useful at the beginning to work with one's particular type. The knowledge seems stunning and the connections almost miraculous. We are amazed at how well the type describes our character. And if we do more than learn our type and its description—in other words, work with the traits and dynamics so that we process and understand them— in time a change occurs. We attain a measure of awareness of ourselves and freedom from the rigidity and narrowness of the type's fixation.

Yet the more we study, the more we notice that the type does not seem to fit as neatly as it did at the beginning. We come to see in our experience and behavior the traits and dynamics of other types. Sometimes it feels as if we are moving around the Enneagram, and we might think our typing is wrong. In time, we might learn that we are actually the totality of the Enneagram. Even though one type will dominate as we begin studying ourselves using the tool of the Enneagram, all the fixations are present in every ego. This becomes apparent as we go deeper in our inner exploration and appreciate the nuances of our inner dynamics. We discover traits that don't fall under the pattern of our primary fixation. This means that if we are genuinely interested in spiritual learning and liberation through the Enneagram, we need to study *all* the fixations—their cores and their shells—as they manifest in our lives. That is how I taught the holy ideas; students learned to work with each point of the Enneagram, exploring the holy idea and the core of each point. I will follow the same methodology in this book. Learning the shell and the key of one's type can unlock the fixation, but having access to all the keys will unravel the totality of the ego, which is patterned by all the fixations.

Facets of Unity presented an understanding of the core of each type's fixation and how unraveling this core leads to the understanding of one's holy idea. This understanding can, in turn, help free one from the constricting neurotic dynamics and problematic traits of the fixation. Such a liberation is a nondual realization of reality. It is a tall order, not easy for many students of the Enneagram. At some point, it occurred to me that my liberation came because I was in possession of the particular key needed to work with the fixation's shell. We each need to understand our shell but also the key to unlock it. This book is a response to that need. We will learn about the key each type needs, and how that key becomes functional in our study and practice.

Most students of the Enneagram, just as all beginning students of any teaching, find themselves in the ordinary world of duality and separateness. It is in this world that we need the keys to the Enneagram, where we are living as our fixated consciousness with no idea how to get out of it, how to liberate that consciousness from its fixation. The keys are needed as tools to work with and navigate this world intelligently and to unravel the fixation so that we can be free and open to other ways the eternal spirit expresses itself. The fixation keeps us in one expression and convinces us that this is the only way reality can be. Even when we relax our fixation (while remaining defined by it), freedom, when it comes, is relative and is still within this world. But freedom from the fixations altogether frees us in a different way; it frees us to move to other manifestations of true nature, and one of these is the nondual world.

There is an interesting conundrum in the nondual view of reality, the view that there are no free agents in the world, no separate beings with their own will and separate mind. How to explain that most people are disconnected from nondual reality? Many nondual teachings explain the disconnection from the nondual as being due to delusions existing in separate, individual minds. But if nonduality is fundamental and true, and separateness is a delusion, then how can an individual be cut off by his or her own beliefs? One resolution to this conundrum is that it is pure consciousness that deludes itself in certain locations. Hence the world of duality is the creation of enlightened consciousness, for where else would it come from when everything is an expression of enlightened consciousness?

The Diamond Approach teaching does not take the view that the ordinary world of people and things, the dualistic reality, is a delusion or is due to individual ignorance. From our perspective, we consider that our spiritual nature—what we usually refer to as true nature—expresses itself in myriad ways. One of these is the nondual way of experiencing, where there is no separateness and, hence, no psychological suffering. But it can also express itself as the ordinary world of duality. It is not an illusion or delusion, but one real expression of the eternal spirit or the unfathomable mystery. It is related to the nondual view, a reflection of it, but this can only be seen from the nondual experience. This ordinary world has its own spirituality. Actually, most human beings experience their spirituality in the ordinary world as some kind of faith, the experience of some spiritual quality, or visionary encounters with spiritual realities.

In the Enneagram, each key to the core of a fixation turns out to be a unique manifestation of pure consciousness or spiritual nature appearing in the world of duality. It is the very substance of nondual consciousness appearing in the world of duality. Finding a key is not a matter of awakening to pure consciousness or awareness, which is a more difficult and rare occurrence. Besides, nondual awakening does not function as the necessary key that each type requires anyway. Most people live in the ordinary world, which nondual teachings refer to as the world of illusion or ignorance. But all practice begins in this ordinary world, and most people live in this dualistic reality. The keys are expressions of enlightened consciousness in the ordinary world—spiritual qualities that embody all that is true and timeless about enlightened awareness—but are particular and manifest locally within the individual and their own experience.

The keys are expressions of the eternal spirit, true and authentic forms of presence manifesting in particular ways without directly challenging duality or necessitating ego death. These forms of presence are much more accessible to us than nondual consciousness or enlightened awareness, precisely because they are meaningful in the ordinary world and quite useful, actually, for navigating our ordinary lives. Similarly, the obstacles to accessing them are also personal and minor in comparison to the obstacles we face trying to access enlightened awareness in its nonduality. In addition, the keys are helpful for any spiritual practice, since they help to unravel the limitations, distortions, and wrong beliefs of the fixation.

We will explore how to work with our fixation in such a way as to find its key. And we will explore each key and how to access it directly and utilize it to free our consciousness from the limitations and distortions of the fixations. Each key spiritual quality is connected to its corresponding holy idea. It is easy to see this connection for some types but more difficult to see it for others. This is because the holy ideas are not qualities or dimensions of our spiritual nature. They are the understanding or wisdom that results from integrating true nature in its nondual expression. But we need to know the many nuances and implications of nonduality that most people miss in order to understand the holy ideas. As that understanding emerges, the connection between the holy ideas and the secret keys to the Enneagram will become more apparent.

Finding and integrating the key for one's particular type opens the door. But passing through it to greater spiritual development and openness requires accessing all nine keys since ego is composed of all the fixations and their delusions, even though one of them predominates. It is when we delve deeper into ourselves that we encounter the other fixations and their cores and the need for all of the secret keys to liberation.

1

THE KEY TO THE ENNEATYPE

This book is not an introduction to the Enneagram or to the Enneagram of fixations. It assumes a basic understanding of the Enneagram, the fixations of each type, and how they develop. You will find it most useful as a complement to the many good books on the subject, such as Sandra Maitri's *The Spiritual Dimension of the Enneagram* or Russ Hudson and Don Riso's *The Wisdom of the Enneagram*. Here I will build upon a basic understanding of the Enneagram with the essential keys that will help free you from the limitations and distortions of each type's fixation. These keys can awaken the power within you that is most effective in loosening the grip of your fixation on your life and your experience. Throughout this book, I will use the words *points* or *types* interchangeably to refer to the Enneagram fixations—*points* referring to the nine points around the circle of the Enneagram symbol and *types* referring to the nine Enneatypes.

I know many students of the Enneagram use it as a personality typology and go no further. This book, however, works with what you know of your type and the Enneagram of fixations in order to open up your inner experience and offer more freedom in your attitudes and actions. The originators of Enneagram knowledge sought to understand reality on all of its levels, in all of its facets, to bring about the ultimate freedom of consciousness. Their primary purpose was spiritual liberation. This book is dedicated to the same endeavor, what is called by some the Great Work.

However deep and profound the knowledge is in my original Enneagram book, *Facets of Unity*, it tends to stay on an intellectual level for many readers. Students of the Enneagram will not find it experientially accessible without the help of a skilled teacher or proficiency in a spiritual practice that reveals personal truth by engaging one's individual experience. My hope is that this book presents more accessible ways to experience the depth of wisdom offered in *Facets of Unity* and at the same time acquaints you with tools that can help you attain a greater capacity for freedom from your fixation.

We are all defined to varying degrees by our type. Some of us are quite fixated on and rigid in unconsciously adhering to the traits and dynamics of our type. Others of us have a looser fixation, as we have done some inner work, either psychological or spiritual, or we were graced with a good enough upbringing. The result is that we have more flexibility and are closer to the essential key of our type. Some of us may already experience the key to our type, with greater freedom from being fixated. Because of this range, I will present the material in a way that speaks to all levels. By including beginners who are more fixated, I can clarify the true outlines for each personality type. You may feel the description doesn't apply to you now; however, it was likely true before you began developing self-awareness, or else you were one of those lucky people who avoided rigid conditioning in childhood. In either case, pointing to the fixated characteristics can help us understand each type in relation to its essential key.

THE CORE AND THE
SHELL OF THE FIXATION

Facets of Unity delineates the holy ideas as an illumination of one of the higher spiritual Enneagrams. It also describes in some detail what happens when limitations in our early childhood experience deny us access to the holy ideas. One of the primary insights is that we are all born with an innate trust in reality, what I term *basic trust*. Depending on how we were held and treated as infants and young children, this trust is impacted, usually diminished, and sometimes seriously broken. The result is what I call the *core* of the type, consisting of three interconnected elements. The painful and difficult emotional state that results from the lack of love and appropriate holding—both physical and emotional—is referred to as the *specific difficulty* for the type. So, each type has, buried deep in the unconscious, a painful and scary internalization of disconnection and lack of holding. Each individual reacts to this state by attempting to veil it, fend it off, or deny or repress it. This I call the *specific reaction*. So for instance, point Three's specific difficulty is helplessness and its specific reaction is striving.

Instead of just being and relaxing in our inner experience of ourselves, as happens when we are lovingly held and cared for, we resort to inner activity. These inner actions are the specific reactions that seek to change our uncomfortable experience. Both the difficulty and the reaction depend on one's type because they reflect the holy idea of each type. As the holding is lost or disrupted and the trust is broken or whittled down, access to the understanding and attitude of the holy idea is lost. We thus lose access to its perspective and wisdom. Because of this, we as children are forced to develop a different idea about reality, a distorted belief that I have termed the *specific delusion* of the type. The delusion is not necessarily a conscious thought for the child, but it is conceptual and implied in both the difficulty and the reaction. In this way, the specific delusion colors the specific difficulty and the specific reaction of each type, thus resulting in nine core complexes. In the complex of point Three, when you believe the delusion that you are a separate doer, the difficulty that is most intolerable is feeling helpless and incapable of doing, and the only remedy seems to be the reaction of constant striving to avoid exposing or feeling the difficulty.

This is a short synopsis of what I call the inner core of the fixation. So, each fixation develops around an inner core, a particular emotional and cognitive complex. (Refer to *Facets of Unity* for greater detail about the core and how it develops, and how basic trust is intimately connected to the goodness inherent in adequate holding.)

The way to work with the core is first to identify the specific reaction in our life and experience. Recognizing and understanding the specific reaction, which attempts to cover up the specific difficulty, can make the specific difficulty visible. This is an emotionally challenging task that makes us feel uncomfortably vulnerable, which is one reason this knowledge probably stays at a mental level for most people. But if we can experience and tolerate the difficulty and the reaction to it, we have a chance of seeing how they are influenced and informed by the specific delusion, which is a particular deeply held belief about reality. Recognizing the specific delusion and understanding it as a delusion and not reality brings us closer to the holy idea of the type, for the delusion functions as a specific barrier to accessing its understanding.

Again using the example of point Three, from this perspective one begins with recognizing the specific reaction—striving— that characterizes the ongoing relationship the Three has with the world. Understanding what the striving is defending against reveals the specific difficulty of helplessness, a very painful inner state of incapacity. As one knows the striving and the helplessness experientially, both elements point to the specific delusion of being a separate doer, the one who has to make things happen. This delusion when recognized as a distorted perspective points to the holy idea that there is only one doer, the Divine Being, the prime mover or what the Mahayana Buddhists refer to as the Buddha of all accomplishing wisdom.

The nine delusions are a particularization of the primary barrier to nondual experience and its realization—the goal of many spiritual teachings. These delusions unpack the main delusion of duality, usually seen as the delusion of separateness or the belief in a separate self. The holy ideas, on the other hand, are ways that we can understand the nondual view. They spell out this view in nine facets, or perspectives. The totality of the nine views, or holy ideas, provides a detailed and comprehensive understanding of the nondual view of reality.

This may seem theoretically somewhat complex, but the real challenge is more emotional than cognitive. In other words, the inner core is difficult to access for it is quite hidden in each type. The core expresses itself indirectly and implicitly as it twists the soul—one's individual consciousness—in a way that determines many things about how the fixation develops.

In fact, what we are aware of when we learn about the Enneagram and identify our type is not the core, but what I call the shell of the fixation. Each fixation has its inner core but also an outer shell that is obvious to others and maybe to ourselves. It takes quite a profound and discriminating awareness—or a great deal of psychological processing—to experience directly and consciously the elements of the core—the specific difficulty and reaction. The specific delusion can be even harder to discern. Part of the difficulty is that the core is obscured by the shell, which is the external part of the fixation, constituting most of its noticeable characteristics. Most people learn about these traits and dynamics through reading about them, not necessarily through direct awareness or understanding.

However, there is a particular dynamic connecting the core to the shell that obscures the elements of the core. Even if we become aware of the specific reaction experientially—a reaction that is an expression of the disruption or limitation of our innate basic trust—the reaction does not usually appear simply as it is. Rather it is camouflaged by a thick network of attitudes, beliefs, relational tendencies, and traits that all imply the reaction while at the same time disguising it. The reaction basically covers up the specific difficulty in order to regain the desired loving holding of reality or of people in our life. But it does so in relation to the specific delusion, the principle that governs the core. This principle is related to our holy idea, but that relationship will not become obvious without an in-depth understanding of spiritual reality, or what I refer to as true nature, as described in *Facets of Unity*.

THE EGO IDEAL

The way we usually feel or know the specific reaction is through each type's ego ideal. Each Enneatype idealizes some way of being or behaving. Trying to attain or approximate this ideal expresses an unconscious wish for it to give us the desired love, safety, and holding of reality and of the important people in our lives. We imagine that we will regain what we lost in childhood or attain what we never had. Continuing with the example of point Three, this type's ego ideal gives inordinate importance to efficiency, success, and achievement.

So, Ego-Go, Oscar Ichazo's original name for point Three on the Enneagram, is constantly striving to be as efficient as possible in order to be successful. This attempt to be like the ego ideal is the primary force that shapes the shell of the type. It is not clear to point Three that their striving is an attempt to cover up a painful deficiency and to regain the fundamental holding of reality. The deficiency, which is related to the specific difficulty of the type, is clearly seen in the Enneagram of avoidances. The avoidances refer to nine behavioral manifestations that each of the nine points prefers to avoid for fear of exposing vulnerability and of undermining the ego ideal (see appendix 3). For point Three, the deficiency we avoid is failure and/or helplessness. The move toward efficiency can be explicit but usually appears as the need to be successful, dependable, and so on, reflecting the other features of the ego ideal in general. More than anything, the ego ideal shapes the patterns of the shell of each type.

Individuals of a given Enneatype share many similarities because they all have the same ego ideal. However, our way of looking up to an ideal and emulating it is highly individual, determined to a large extent by our early childhood and the dynamics of our early relationships. So not all point Three individuals are the same. The differences are dictated by their early upbringing, experiences in life, social environment and influences, and innate physical and psychological dispositions. And their culture and life situations also have an influence.

Understanding and unraveling the shell requires recognizing our ego ideal and how we attempt to emulate it or be it as closely as possible. Freud recognized early on (and Western depth psychology concurs) that inherent in every ego structure is an ego ideal. But the science of the Enneagram has gone a step further to say that there are nine principal ego ideals that pattern all egos. Thus, each type always has its own ideal way to be.

Identifying our ego ideal is not that difficult if we study our fixation. I can list the ego ideal of each type (refer to appendix 3), but this is simply information; we need to experience them in action in our lives. The ego ideal is a view or image of ourselves that we are attempting to actualize. Words can point to it, but our self-study is what makes it possible for us to experience it as living knowledge. Even so, the ego ideal is not the key that we need to unravel the fixation and its hold on us. That key is the esoteric secret taught in the Diamond Approach and revealed in this book.

Remember that the wisdom of the Sarmoun, the original ancient source of the Enneagram knowledge, runs as one of the currents in the logos of this teaching. By applying the knowledge of the Diamond Approach to the Enneagram, I had the inspired revelation of the holy ideas that I wrote about in *Facets of Unity* and, with it, how the specific reaction expresses itself in the shell of the type through the ego ideal. This latter revelation has now become the basis of this book, *Keys to the Enneagram*. When I applied the knowledge of the Diamond Approach, what occurred was a spontaneous revelation, or inspired knowing, that took into consideration all that I had known and then synthesized it all into new insights into the Enneagram—here specifically related to the recognition of the ego ideal and how it forms.

ONE'S UNIQUE ESSENTIAL ENDOWMENT

The insight into the ego ideal of each type is that it is a facsimile, an imitation of something else, at best an approximation of something real and authentic that is beyond ego. The ego ideal does not simply arise out of our conditioning. Nor do we learn it from idealizing somebody else. It is not born from our longing to be like our childhood hero. In fact, it is the other way around: we find the hero who corresponds to our ideal. What I saw was that we were not only born with one holy idea being dominant but also with a particular quality of pure consciousness or true nature.

In this path, the inner spiritual truth inherent to all beings is referred to as true nature. True nature is more subtle and more innate than what most people think of as spirit. Spirit is usually seen as distant and of another world. In this teaching, *spirit* is nothing but an old term for what I refer to as our true nature, the true nature of our consciousness, the consciousness that makes experience possible. There are many ways of viewing or experiencing this true nature, depending on the path. In this path, the emphasis is on recognizing true nature as the presence of Being, as the being of our consciousness. The presence of Being, or the being of consciousness, appears in many forms that we call qualities, or aspects. So it is not simply presence but the presence of love or the presence of intelligence, and so on.

Within this context, we recognize that we are each born with one quality of true nature, or essential presence. This quality of authentic spiritual presence is related to the holy idea in an interesting way. This connection expresses how the spirituality of nonduality relates to the spirituality of the ordinary dual world. The important insight is that we are born with one quality of Being, or authentic presence, as a particular essential endowment, which means we can access it more easily than the others. In many cases we experience it as children without knowing it; later all that remains is some feeling of it, some appreciation of how it affected us.

This feeling—whether intuitive or unconscious—combined with our appreciation of the quality's characteristics becomes the nucleus of our ego ideal. Thus, the ego ideal imitates the essential quality. We try to be someone who embodies this quality, but we don't know the quality of presence directly and consciously. We just have a sense—an intuition of it or of some of its main characteristics. This becomes what we idealize, what forms the ego ideal for our type's fixation. In other words, as the shell develops, rather than embodying the essential quality, we end up idealizing a facsimile of it. The shell develops around the idealization, which is a shadow of the quality, not the true quality. We develop a shell around our core instead of realizing the quality that can help us penetrate the core and dissolve it.

Point Three is always striving to be efficient and functionally successful because true efficiency and functionality are two of the characteristics associated with the essential quality of this type. The quality is what gives us efficiency or the capacity to be efficient— but in the right way and for the right purpose or action—because the quality is authentic and has many other characteristics that we will see reflected in some way in Ego-Go. Ego-Go is efficient in doing, in becoming successful, in being recognized as the desired ideal in ordinary materialistic society. But the true essential quality gives us the opportunity to be a true human being, a person who lives life effectively while being an expression of Being. The point is not to be the ideal for the particular society we happen to be born into but to be our unique authentic personhood, a person of Being who is both efficiently functional and grounded in Being. Truth dominates instead of the self-deception that results from pursuing the ego ideal.

There are two ways of accessing our unique essential endowment, which is the quality of Being, or the eternal spirit that our ego ideal tries to emulate. One is through the ego ideal. By seeing and understanding our particular ego ideal, we approach the essential quality it is trying to emulate. By understanding how the ego ideal patterns our personality on the one hand and how the characteristics and traits of our personality reflect the essential quality on the other, we may be able to recognize the quality itself. But it is only when we know that our ego ideal is not the real thing—that it is a facsimile, a conceptual approximation, just an idea or picture in our mind—that we can have the openness, the space for that essential quality to arise. This means we need to see that our ego ideal is a fake reality constructed from intuitions and obscure feelings combined with conditioned patterns from our early upbringing and cultural programming.

By seeing the fake and conceptually constructed idea that forms the ideal, we can come face to face with the real Platonic idea that is the essential quality. We can then recognize that what we are trying to be is something we already have, a quality of our being that we can access directly. We can see it is not a construct, but an authentic presence, a form that the eternal spirit—our true nature—takes. When we become acquainted with this presence and, even better, realize it and know it as what we are, then it can become the greatest help. Realizing this presence becomes the most effective tool for unwinding our fixation and penetrating the core. We begin to understand and appreciate our particular holy idea and how it frees us from the limitations and distortions of our fixation.

The second way to access our essential endowment is more direct. It involves utilizing the knowledge and wisdom of the Diamond Approach to open up to our being and recognize this essential presence. We can draw on a basic teaching of this path called the theory of holes. (See chapter 2 in *Diamond Heart Book One* and chapter 3 in *Essence.* to get a fuller understanding of the theory of holes.) It presupposes that we are born still able to access our spiritual nature. We are connected to its qualities without knowing it and express them innocently. This is one reason why we love children and find babies adorable: they are endearing because they are innocently transparent to the wonderful world of spirit with its love, joy, peace, and so on.

Going through the rough-and-tumble of life and the difficulties of childhood interrupts and eventually blocks access to our true being. It happens in some general ways but also in specific ways that are related to each particular aspect, or quality, of true nature. Whenever our access or openness to a particular quality is obstructed, we feel disconnected from it. We are usually not conscious of this process when we are young, but some children can be aware of it to a certain degree. Later on, when we experience the disconnection from a particular quality, we feel an absence, a lack, which is an emptiness that has the affect of missing that specific quality. The lack for type Three feels like failure. We call this state of specific disconnection a hole, for we can notice it experientially as a deficient emptiness in our body; in truth, something is missing in our consciousness. Encountering this kind of disconnection and staying with it can lead us directly to the experience of the missing quality. (You can find examples of this process in many of my other books, including *Essence* and *The Void*.)

There is a relationship between your particular aspect and your particular holy idea. If you are familiar with the latter, you may get a sense of what the connection is as you read the following chapters. However, in this book my focus is not on this particular relationship.

The sequence of Enneatypes in the following chapters does not follow any particular flow of the Enneagram, inner or outer. I chose the order based on the essential qualities for each type, addressing the qualities that are easiest to access first and leaving the more subtle ones for last. My intention is to make the material as accessible as possible experientially so that you can reconnect with your particular aspect, the quality of presence that is the key to unraveling your fixation.

ARE WE ONLY OUR TYPE?

It is important to remember that each ego self contains all the types. One type dominates, but when we investigate this type deeply, we find that our personality also includes all the other fixations. In other words, the ego self has all nine fixations, all nine delusions, in its inner core. By exploring each fixation as it appears in our sense of self, we may access its idealized aspect. This means it is possible for us to access nine idealized qualities by studying our fixated ego self, which in turn will make penetrating the inner core of our type much easier since we have many powerful qualities of presence to aid us. It is rare that an individual will access all nine of the idealized aspects, and I am not saying we need to do this in order to be able to penetrate our inner core. But the more essential qualities we integrate, the easier it is for us to open up the core of our type and access its holy idea. In fact, there is the potential for us to penetrate the cores of all nine types and access all their holy ideas. In this way, the Enneagram map functions as a powerful tool for spiritual realization and liberation.

2

Point Eight
TRUE STRENGTH

Each ego idealization patterns the type so pervasively that it colors, even determines, many of its traits, attitudes, and preferences. We start with point Eight, Ichazo's Ego-Venge (also called the Challenger), because its ego ideal is easiest to understand, and its idealized aspect is the most accessible to the average person. Ego-Venge's fixation is more obvious than other types because overt aggression characterizes its expression. Eights can be easily angered and use belligerence as a primary mode of relating to the world. They are often boisterous, loud, bullying, and more inclined to fight things out than other types. Naranjo writes: "Related to the characteristic of hostility of the ennea-type is dominance. . . . Related to dominance are such traits as 'arrogance,' 'power seeking,' 'need for triumph,' 'putting others down,' 'competitiveness,' 'acting superior.'"[1] Eight's idealization, according to Naranjo, is "I am powerful, I can do." This is a close approximation of the idealized aspect. Of course, not all Eights have such coarse manifestations; many are simply assertive and strong and find the emotion of anger easily available to them. However, our intention is to highlight the Enneatypes in their rawness, for this is what clarifies the idealized quality.

It is not unusual for Eights to be physically large. However, even if they are not physically big, Eights act big by employing outsized gestures and expressions and by being loud and assertive. They take up space. They can be uncouth, rough, unabashed in public, fearless, and even shameless in expressing themselves or making their needs known. Much to the embarrassment of family and friends, they can be forcefully demanding and use vulgar language or act in a vulgar way in social situations. A good example of someone demonstrating this trait was Fritz Perls, the German analyst who coined the term "Gestalt therapy." He was an expansive Eight who was known to not care about whether he was socially appropriate.

Naturally, type Eight has other qualities—such as defending the weak and helpless, especially the victimized—but I am emphasizing character traits that most clearly reflect the ego ideal. For instance, rather than refer to their willingness to fight for justice, I am pointing to the extremes to which they'll go to achieve it, including the use of vengeance and cruelty. Further, this vengeance and cruelty is not always in the service of justice or defense of the victimized. They can merely be reactions to others' perceived insults and humiliations.

The ego ideal for point Eight is strength and the aggression related to it. Many of the character traits mentioned so far express strength and assertive aggression in one way or another. But we can understand these traits more clearly if we have some idea of the true essential quality this strength is emulating.

IDEALIZED ASPECT: TRUE STRENGTH

Point Eight's idealized strength is an approximation, a poor imitation of true strength. It perceives strength physically or socially as brute strength or strength of character. But this is strength as seen from the animal point of view, where we feel we are in command, the top dog, or the unchallenged leader of the pack. This strength is sometimes expressed in extreme ways, as in the case of Joseph Stalin, who displayed unimaginable excesses of brutality and aggression, and Saddam Hussein. A more mature and moderate example of an Eight is Winston Churchill, who stood courageously against Nazi aggression and led Britain in the dark years of the Second World War until victory was achieved. More recently, Margaret Thatcher, the Iron Lady, was an Eight who stared down widespread opposition as she remade the British social contract through austerity and breaking the power of the unions, among other things.

These character traits give us a feel for an expansive strength that—when distorted by ego—can become vulgar, offensive, and cruel, resulting in bullies and ruthless dictators. Teasing out the essential quality requires seeing the positive and truly effective *constructive* expression of aggression. We must go beyond what appears nonhuman, unacceptable, and not useful—what is destructive and dysfunctional—to reveal the positive quality the ego is trying to emulate. Of course, different Eights express the essential quality of strength in different ways with varying degrees of distortion, imitation, or approximation. Only with careful observation can we discern the common elements that, in their totality, point to what is real behind the fixated manifestations.

PRESENCE OF TRUE STRENGTH

The true quality behind the Eight's ego ideal is the actual essence of aggression, the positive and useful function of authentic assertive strength. But because Eights do not truly know this quality or embody it, they go to great lengths to emulate it, striving to be strong in an egoic or primitive animal way. What are the true characteristics of real strength, the Being?

First, all essential qualities are states of Being with characteristics that emanate from the authentic presence of Being. We know them by immediately experiencing them in our bodies, in our consciousness, as a fullness or presence that is not physical. I am not referring to the ordinary meaning of being, as in being present with a focus of attention or awareness. Instead, we experience ourselves as a kind of medium or substance, a continuum that is not a physical sensation but actually consciousness feeling itself directly as a pooling that senses its own presence throughout the entire medium uniformly. It knows itself as that medium without being informed from the outside or by any remembered knowledge. This is unusual in ordinary experience, for our consciousness is usually not aware of itself but of something else, such as emotions, sensations, thoughts, external objects, or phenomena—all manifestations of consciousness. Here it is subjectivity feeling itself, recognizing its own being. It is intimate and completely immediate. It's likely you've had some sense of this realm of experiencing, or some intimations or glimpses of it. But it is a whole *world* of experiencing, and we can explore some of it by knowing the idealized aspects.

Nowadays, when teachers talk of consciousness that is conscious of itself, they usually mean pure consciousness absent of qualities. From that perspective, it is infinite and boundless, pervading everything. This is the nondual way consciousness wakes up to itself, the presence of pure consciousness or awareness. While this is real and true, if we believe consciousness can only be this way, we deprive ourselves of the variety and richness of the mystery of consciousness. We can experience it in so many other ways that are authentic and useful for ordinary living at the same time. In the ordinary world of duality, consciousness can be conscious of itself in a local way, as in our body—belly or chest. In this sense, it can feel localized and not infinite, as a medium that fills the belly or the whole body without pervading everything. It might take form as a flow, a pool, a ball, or a shape of any kind. The salient point about spiritual experience in the ordinary world (in contradistinction to the nondual world) is that it is localized and particular, with a form and often a color, a taste, and a texture as well.

What is most important for knowing the idealized qualities is that presence is not only consciousness that is conscious of its being, but also conscious of this being manifesting itself with a particular quality. This is something nondual teachings often ignore and many nondual teachers might not know in experience.

When we experience true strength, we feel strong because we are feeling the presence of strength itself—we are full of an energy and presence that is the essence of the life force. The most common experience is to perceive heat in the lower body, like fire that does not burn. It can appear visually as a flame or as a raging fire, red and luminous. True strength is a medium that is self-luminous, not only with awareness and sensitivity, but with a beautiful and magnificent ruby red light. This fiery red presence has a particular, unmistakable affect: the affect of strength. We feel strong because we are touched by or filled with the essence of strength. It is not physical or animal, not muscular or emotional, but organic and innate, part of what we are. It is not something that we possess but rather a quality of who we are, of our own consciousness, an aspect of our being.

In addition to a fire or flame, red strength may appear as flowing lava, a dense liquid coursing through the pelvis, legs, or the whole body. It can also be a red bloodlike fluid pulsing through the body and consciousness. Luminous and conscious of itself, it is a fluid of sensitivity that innately has the feeling of strength—strength of being, strength of spirit.

When first becoming aware of the essence of strength, many do not recognize that it is the presence of strength sensing and knowing itself. We tend to believe that we, as the ego personality, are feeling and knowing it. It takes curiosity and discernment to realize that we do not usually experience and know strength this way. The knowing of strength comes from the presence itself; it does not come from learned knowledge. Strength has its own sensing; we as selves are not sensing it. This is a revelation in its own right, revealing the dimension of direct knowing, or gnosis.

Strength is innate and fundamental and comprises the platonic form that informs all other kinds of strength—physical, emotional, mental, moral and so on. It is the prototype of strength on any level, but it is also strength that is pure and on its own, not the strength of something but presence as strength. As I have mentioned, this true strength may appear in many forms, but no matter how strength appears it is frequently hot and always a beautiful ruby red, pure and unearthly in its color and pure in its affect of strength. When this presence arises, we feel we are here and present, but also strong. If we sense it completely and nondualistically—meaning we are inseparable from its presence within our individual consciousness—we feel we *are* the presence of strength, pure strength, the very essence of strength.

Most humans know the common quality of physical or emotional strength, but few are aware that it has a spiritual origin, a heavenly counterpart. Now we see how this idealized aspect connects with the ego ideal. The latter is the common strength and assertive aggression that most people know without recognizing that their experience is a reflection and, hence, a distortion of something much more real and authentic, an actual presence.

CHARACTERISTICS
OF TRUE STRENGTH

The presence of strength has many associated characteristics, which impact our individual consciousness, our soul. (In our work, we use the terms *soul* and *individual consciousness* interchangeably to mean the usual conscious subjective field we experience, but one with more dimensions than we are usually aware of.) These characteristics further illuminate the traits of point Eight.

Strength, the fiery energy and presence that we feel, can appear as the life force itself. This is because the life force includes this essential strength, though it also includes energy and dynamic creative aliveness. So when experiencing strength we are often struck by how alive we feel, as if we are teeming with life, as if aliveness has woken up throughout our body and being. We can feel we are robust life itself. Strength inherently has robustness and vitality, infusing the life force with its potent vibrancy. This is the essential source of the boisterous and loud traits characterizing the Eight, and it explains their tendency to express themselves with vigor and unbridled energy. But because the fixated type is not aware of essential strength, it models itself on a facsimile of strength, appearing as loudness and boisterousness that is not always called for or appropriate. It is vigor and vitality expressed in a distorted way.

Another associated characteristic we may experience with essential strength is the sense of expansion. We feel big in comparison to how we usually feel, bigger than our body, bigger than other people, even bigger than the room. There is no limit to how expanded we can feel, and this brings spaciousness and freedom, the absence of constrictions in mind and heart. Since point Eight is not in touch with this authentic expansion of being, the big feeling is often unconsciously understood as some sense of self-importance. They act expansively by taking up space with their physical energy and loudness, with uninhibited and capacious expression. Their belief that they have no limitations, however, is usually not true unless they are somebody in a position of power like Stalin or Hussein, whose expansion took sinister turns at the expense of many other human beings. This was not the expansion or expression of true strength because that strength disappears when the action of ego tries to direct it for unwholesome ends.

Both strength and expansion fuel a sense of courage and spontaneous boldness that makes us truly fearless in the face of difficulties and challenges, dangers and threats (real or imaginary). The example of Churchill is apt here. We are not hindered by conventional limits. Courage is not reserved for the battlefield but available for all the continuing battles of life, where we must confront challenging situations or difficult people in ways that work and that result in real effectual consequences. We are bold in being ourselves and expressing our authenticity, not cowering or passive, not held back or small in word and deed. The degree of boldness and courage we manifest will depend on how much we have integrated real strength into our sense of who we are. Eights frequently exhibit a fearlessness that lacks this deeper source and thus has a tendency to be expressed in socially inappropriate or destructive ways.

This brings us to the central issue of both the Eight character and the idealized aspect of strength: the question of aggression. Eights tend to be aggressive as evidenced in rough and tough speech and actions, sometimes sharp and insensitive but also lively and stimulating. However, this ordinary aggressiveness can devolve into a highly destructive trait, cruel and inhuman, as happens with many despots and tyrants. These individuals are extreme and reflect a distorted sense of what true aggression is, which is part of the strength aspect of essence.

When we integrate essential strength—the ruby fire, lava, or presence—we experience a sense of capacity, a feeling of "I can." The sense of capacity that accompanies expansion and courage becomes the ability to assert oneself in fullness and honesty, to affirm one's truth without hesitation or limitation. We can assert ourselves in all our relationships, whether with loved ones or authority figures, friends or family—anywhere that we need to stand up for ourselves—and our assertion will make those relationships healthier. It needn't be loud or rough, but bold and solid. It can even be gentle and kind but assertive nevertheless in that it is not a retreat or a holding back, it is not contracting into oneself. Such assertion, expansion, courage, and fire of spirit constitute the true aggression.

However, the word *aggression* has more often had negative connotations. There was a time when psychoanalysts struggled to conjure a word that implied aggression that was not destructive or angry. One result was "neutralized aggression," but this is inadequate to describe the true aggression of Being. We might call it aggressiveness, or simply courageous assertiveness. But it is also expansive and can become explosive in the service of truth, destroying falsehood and lies. It can enlist anger if it is in the service of good ends, not just for oneself but for all others. That is why some realized people express anger, usually referred to as wrath. But wrath is a far cry from the anger and aggression that characterizes the Eight's fixation in its extreme or raw expressions, where anger is more often fury and rage in the service of revenge, energy that can turn into cruelty and brutality. Most of the time, however, the fixation's aggression is just bothersome—not to the point, not useful, just hurtful. It is reactive anger, automatic and conditioned, not sensitive or attuned. This is the anger of Ego-Venge, very different from the anger of the sage, which expresses itself as a might of Being that challenges unconsciousness and limited views. Even when fiery and destructive, it is in the service of truth.

Investigating the approximations of true strength in the ego ideal of the Eight can point us toward the true quality of essence. Integrating this strength is quite helpful for life's challenges but also for our spiritual practices and explorations, because we cannot traverse a true spiritual path without being lionhearted, without embodying true strength. It helps all of us in unraveling our own fixation and in penetrating the deep core that holds it together. The realization of true strength liberates us from the outer shell of the type and readies us for tackling the more interior task of working out the inner core to reach a greater freedom.

THE DIRECT APPROACH
TO TRUE STRENGTH

While understanding the Eight ego ideal can point to essential strength, it is not the easiest or most direct path. Certain spiritual practices can lead more directly and completely to its experience and integration. One of the simplest methods is the tantric approach, which refers to the use and transformation of energy for the sake of evolving spiritual being. Energy can be erotic, even sexual, or it can be emotional, mental, or simply energy itself. Whether we are a type Eight or not, when we feel angry or vengeful the tantric practice is not to act it out or express it by yelling, blaming, or cursing anybody. Instead, we sense the feeling of anger or rage and stay with it in its purity. We don't try to change or suppress it. We do not side with our justifications for it or listen to our stories about it.

We just feel our anger in our body, as completely as possible, while containing it so the energy does not seep out or dissipate.

If we feel the anger this way, it reveals itself to be a strong energy that is aggressive and bristling. Over time, by not expressing it, we can recognize the source of this energy and instead of the affect feeling prickly, we experience it as a fiery quality. If we stay with it longer and repeatedly—making it a practice, in other words—we end up experiencing it as the presence of strength with its courage and expansiveness. We might not recognize it as presence at the beginning, but we can recognize the sense of heat, energy, and expansiveness that feels natural and organic, even primordial. To know the sense of presence takes more discrimination of what this strength is exactly.

The practice that is more specific to this teaching is exploring certain sectors of the personality that are related to the disconnection from true strength. The central one is feeling the state of weakness that we assume must be there if we are not able to access true strength. Weakness is the trait of type Eight mentioned in the Enneagram of avoidances, and it implies the disconnection from the presence of strength, which means there are obstacles in its way. Type Eight individuals abhor feeling weak. But that is exactly where they need to go in order to regain the connection with their essential endowment. Actually, the bristling anger, the loud exuberance, and the unbridled aggression frequently hide this feeling of weakness. This is how Eights fend off weakness and fight against feeling it.

Truly understanding our type to the point of spiritual illumination requires motivation and the love for reality and truth. These are what allow us to be willing to open to our vulnerability, which is necessary to confront the underlying state of weakness. First, however, we need to see all the ways we avoid feeling weak.

The avoidance covers up the weakness and points our attention away such that we are not even aware of feeling weak. There can be many ways we do this, and they depend on the individual rather than the type. We learn these avoidance strategies in early childhood as we interact with the important people in our environment. Two ways these might still manifest in adulthood are denying our weakness or vulnerability even when we feel it and compensating for our vulnerability with anger so we feel strong.

To be able to engage in this exploration into our fear of weakness and vulnerability, we must first develop our capacity to sense our body and what happens in it. Perceiving the sensations in our body is not an easy matter at the beginning. Most people sense their body only superficially, with many areas completely out of awareness. Only by focusing attention on the individual parts of our body can we learn to feel it completely, and without this full-bodied awareness, we cannot recognize the patterns manifesting in it. Gradually relaxing and letting go of tension patterns that we have developed throughout our life will, over time, allow us to freely sense our body. This ability to sense the body completely, deeply, and fully, exactly as it is in the moment, is a practice all on its own that supports knowing the immediacy of presence.

We also need to develop our capacity to feel by exploring what prevents us from experiencing our emotions—or, at least, the particular emotions we defend against. This again is part of spiritual practice and discipline. We can develop awareness by practicing mindfulness, but it can remain mental if we do not feel our emotions. To be able to feel our emotions deeply and fully requires our heart to be open and unobstructed by patterns of emotional conflict or defenses against hurt, fear, loneliness, and so on. Opening our heart as completely as spiritual practice requires can be a difficult and painful process. Yet it is possible, and the process transforms us into true human beings.

By the time we have accessed all the idealized aspects, our bodies will have become transparent to presence and our hearts open and receptive to experiencing the affects that reflect the various qualities of presence. We will have developed our capacity to sense and to be consciously embodied, since this is necessary for that transparency to occur. And our hearts will be willing and able to feel any emotion that arises, regardless of type or intensity.

This willingness of the heart is what allows us to feel the bare, undefended state of weakness. Justifying or explaining it, covering it up or denying it, suppressing or limiting it is the action of the ego attempting to reject this very real part of our experience. Instead, we embrace the weakness and helplessness as a precious gift. It is our doorway to our authentic being. As we feel the state of weakness without defending against it or trying to change it, something new happens.

By acknowledging the truth of our underlying feeling of weakness, we become open to the truth that lies beyond it, the truth of true strength. We realize that the weakness has some kind of emptiness we can feel in our belly or pelvis or sometimes along the right side of the body. The state of weakness, since it is due to the disconnection from true strength, is both the feeling of disconnection and the affect that reflects the absence of the quality. In other words, the state of weakness naturally and spontaneously becomes—if we stop our manipulations—the deficient state of having no strength. We feel the disconnection as a lack, as an emptiness characterized by the feeling of having no strength. Instead of feeling weak, we feel "I do not have strength." This feeling that strength is not here is the state of disconnection, which turns out to be a state of deficient emptiness. Some people are familiar with emptiness of this kind and some are not. If it is not familiar, this feeling of "something is missing" might scare us. Nevertheless, the feeling is real and we need to feel this sense of something missing.

The deficient emptiness can bring up situations from our past that led to the disconnection—painful early childhood experiences with one of our parents or siblings or somebody important at that time. The dynamics that led to the disconnection become apparent, and the more that we know, see, and feel them completely, the more we understand those dynamics and how they affect our current situation. This understanding is precious as well as necessary for the next step, which is the actual arising of the missing state of presence.

As we acquaint ourselves with this emptiness and feel comfortable enough in it that we can stop resisting it, it changes on its own. It becomes a state of spaciousness, an openness that is clear and clean. Within this openness the presence of true strength can arise. It can be a heat or fire in the belly or a flow of red-hot strength. We might feel strong with a sense of capacity and boldness, or we might feel the sense of true presence characterized by strength. Thus we have moved through the specific hole of strength, the gateway to being that I described in chapter 1 as the theory of holes.

Continuing to work on the obstacles to weakness, or to strength itself, through understanding our early dynamics, we gain more access to true strength, and we also integrate this state of Being as one of the qualities of our present consciousness. This means we have found the key to unlocking the knot of the Eight's fixation. But we have also acquired a strength that will be useful in our life, in our spiritual practices in general, and in dealing with the core of other types. Most important of all, we have entered the dimension of spirit by embodying the true presence of spirit, arising here as the essence and source of strength in all its dimensions. We now know what presence is—meaning we have recognized our spiritual nature—and we know what true strength is. It is a strength that does not fade or decrease. It can only expand and deepen, and it gives our life greater vigor, aliveness, and expansiveness. That expansion can become unstoppable and endless if we continue in our spiritual journey.

I have discussed how to access the essential quality of strength in some detail to illustrate how the recovery of our essence occurs. We see how the theory of holes helps us to directly access the quality. In future chapters, I won't be going through all of these details for each type, but the process is similar. It is the terrain—the specific issues and historical patterns that block our access to each quality—that varies.

3

Point Six
PERSONAL WILL

The indications of the ego ideal patterning in point Six lie in one of two categories: phobic or counterphobic. Both express the ego ideal, but the phobic Six does not feel successful in approximating it while the counterphobic does. Both reflect the idealized aspect and point to it. However, it is not easy to recognize the reflection if we have no idea what the idealized aspect is or what some of its characteristics are, because the latter do not always correspond to conventional knowledge the way type Eight characteristics do.

The traits that are relevant for us are those of stubbornness, hardheadedness, unyielding determination, and a refusal to listen to others. When relating to authority or parental figures, these traits manifest as rebelliousness, an insistence on having one's way, and obstinate persistence in spite of opposition or challenges.

The counterphobic Six tends to oppose authority—being rebellious, suspicious, fearful, and even paranoid, as well as self-reliant, sometimes to an unrealistic degree. The phobic type Six (Ego-Cow in Ichazo's parlance and also known as the Loyalist) tends to revere authority—committing to it in a sustained way, which can become compliance, sometimes to the point of subservience. Phobic Sixes can also show respect, adoration, loyalty, and deference to authority, which can be laudable qualities but can go to extremes, even to the point of giving up choice and self-determination. Naranjo writes:

> Just as it is true that at the psychological level proper the ennea-type VI individual gives up his power before authority, it is also possible to say that it is the very sense of being that is given up through its projection upon individuals, systems, or ideas endowed with a "greater than life" importance or sublimity.[1]

Both counterphobic and phobic Sixes crave security and safety, and they need to rely on something solid—an authority figure, a cause, an organization, or one's belief in one's opinions and decisions. Indecision and stuttering in their behavior and attitude also reflect the ego ideal in that they feel they are not measuring up to it. This also appears in fearfulness and a tendency toward anxiety and uncertainty. Jiddu Krishnamurti began life as a phobic Six, very obedient to his theosophical masters in his younger years. After his transformation, however, he rebelled, becoming a kind of awakened Six who nevertheless did not overcome his fixation. He had the steadiness of will, but opposed authority of any kind, often unrealistically, regardless of the clarity of his realization. But he was definitely a transformed Six, not controlled by fears, paranoia, or projections. At the extreme of this type we have Hitler, who embodied the suspicious, paranoid character in need of possessing all authority, and we know how far he went in believing he was the sole authority on earth.

THE IDEALIZED ASPECT:
PERSONAL WILL

All these traits and tendencies, styles of behavior, and patterns of reaction can easily be explained by the true quality of being that the ideal is trying to approximate or imitate. True personal will possesses some similarities to the conventional understanding of will, but it goes much further than this familiar sense. This is the reason it is difficult to discriminate the idealized aspect from the patterns of the shell of this type's fixation.

The type Six idea of will is more akin to willfulness and what is commonly known as an unbreakable will, which can be so inflexible and hard that, when idealized, it is referred to as an "iron" will. Many consider an iron will to be a good quality. However, this iron quality makes a person defensive and inflexible, even insensitive and inhuman. It also appears as hardheadedness. We can confidently say that Hitler had an iron will because he persistently exercised ruthless authority and did so at the expense of many victims whom he suspected or feared. This reflected the fact that he was disconnected from true will and most likely was suffering from a sense of castration and deficiency that he defended against with an unrelenting dedication to power and authority, a dedication that could not deviate or retreat, change course or yield. Of course, most Sixes are not like Hitler, but we are using his example to show in caricature how far this distortion of personal will can go. Most Sixes have a distortion of personal will but in various degrees, some of them coming close to true will. The term we use in our teaching to refer to this kind of defensive determination is "false" will. When we find ourselves willful in an intractable and insensitive way, we can actually sense in our solar plexus an iron ball that is hard and unyielding. Though solid and impenetrable, it is a poor imitation of true will. False will is unrealistically exaggerated and unhelpful for learning and inner development or for serving others and their well-being.

PRESENCE OF PERSONAL WILL

Just as there are many ways we can experience essential strength, there are various ways we can experience personal will, which is the key to freedom from the fixation for point Six. Any essential presence can be experienced in various degrees of subtlety and refinement, each reflecting a particular level of realization or depth of experience. Some people first encounter personal will as a "full moon" in the area of the solar plexus, similar to how some Sufis look at this quality. This full moon is a luminous silver white like the moon in the sky and is experienced as having lightness with some density. It feels like a disc of condensed silver white light that makes us confident and centered, determined and steadfast. We can already see how some of the shell traits are attempts to mimic these true, pure qualities. By being stubborn and willful, the Six is attempting to simulate the qualities of determination and steadfastness that go with the confidence that originates from one's true being. Both phobic and counterphobic Sixes lack true confidence, but each reacts to this lack differently.

This first arising of will is most often a subtle white presence or substance. The full moon tends to arise when the center for this aspect opens in the solar plexus. At this level it is one of what the Sufis call the *lataif*, or "subtleties." They believe the white presence, will, is the first *latifa* (the singular form of lataif) to be activated because it acts as a bridge to the spiritual world, and it is associated in their system with the prophet Moses. (In the Sufi system, there are usually five lataif with their own centers: white at the solar plexus, yellow above the left nipple, red above the right nipple, black at the center of the forehead, and green at the center of the chest, or heart center. We will refer to these on occasion, but the Diamond Approach is different from the Sufi system, even though it sees the colors and centers the way the Sufis see them.) The full moon quickly becomes the white latifa, or white subtle presence. It also has a sense of centeredness and a kind of will that is not willful but flexible, responding and adapting according to our needs or the needs and demands of the situation.

The most characteristic and frequent experience of personal will is as the presence of silver, either liquid or solid. This level is more substantial than the white latifa. Silver reflects the fact that it is softer and hence more flexible than the hard rigidity of iron. Here the sense of presence is most clear; it is a density of subtle presence, usually a concentrated mass of pure silver consciousness filling the belly or lower body. When silver is solid it is usually stationary and localized in the body, but when it is flowing as a liquid, it can go anywhere in the body according to the functional need or inner state.

In addition to a solid silver ball in the solar plexus or belly, the presence can also be sensed as a column that fills the spine, giving us the feeling that we "have a backbone," as the expression goes. Or it may appear as a solid mass filling the lower body with the sense of immensity and solidity of a mountain. In fact, this experience of silver is the living presence of solidity. Presence often reveals itself as some kind of spacious expanse but here it manifests as a solid mass with its own perception and knowing of itself. It is a mass that is sensitive and aware throughout its entire field, whether solid or liquid. This sensitivity recognizes its own presence and the quality of malleable silver solidity that is distinctive to the presence of personal will. This essential silver will is shimmering and luminous in contrast to the iron will, which tends to feel dark and heavy—sometimes even rusty and old—like cast iron.

Many who know presence from experience know it as a sense of fullness or substantiality that is not physical. The substantiality indicates the reality and existence of consciousness or being. It feels true and real, and we feel present and authentically ourselves. Yet we might not be aware that presence has many qualities and that it can be experienced as solid or liquid silver. Hard silver has the same sense we experience physically: metallic and cool. While iron feels metallic, it is not pleasant, having a hardness that is unresponsive and an immovability that can feel stuck. Conversely, silver feels alive, sensitive, and conscious of itself, and the metallic quality is comforting, comfortable, and easy. Even the liquid silver has a solidity of presence, where we feel definite and immediate, rooted and grounded, without being swayed by the vagaries of time and circumstance.

It is also possible to feel the whole body as solid silver, as if we are a living statue of silver, gleaming and clean, pure with a sense of virginity and pristineness. And yet we can move easily and smoothly, for this solid silver, while not physical, gives the physical an inner support for its stance and movement. This body of silver is presence that is conscious of its solidity or liquidity and knows itself as firm and strong. It also knows itself as personal will. This knowing comes from the presence itself, not from the mind, for the mind might never have known will this way.

We see here something important about presence and its knowledge, different from the conventional experience of external objects or emotional and mental states. The experience of presence and the knowing that it is presence are the same. The knowing and the being are one—a characteristic of gnosis in general, which is the spiritual mode of knowing. In other words, the knowing is not a mental remembering or deduction.

Here, since we are experiencing a particular quality of presence, the knowing is of the presence of will. So being the sensation of solidity and knowing it as solid will go together; they are inseparable. We can feel it and sense it with this knowing. We can sense the texture, smoothness, and coolness of the silver, even the silver taste. Nobody has to tell us it is presence or that it is the presence of true will, and nobody can sway us from that knowing. For in this knowing there is the certainty of gnosis. This is true of our experience of presence in general, and when the experience is sufficiently complete, it is true of experiencing all essential aspects or qualities.

CHARACTERISTICS OF PERSONAL WILL

Now we want to see how the personal will relates to the traits of the fixation's shell. We detect the characteristics of true will partly through its texture and sensations but mostly by the way it impacts our consciousness. By consciousness here I mean our individual consciousness, not universal or cosmic consciousness. It is also what I refer to as our individual soul. Cosmic consciousness is what we discussed in *Facets of Unity*, and it is relevant for understanding the holy ideas. It is not what we need as the key to the type.

Solidity is one way this aspect feels; it is the direct experience of silver presence. It should be noted that solidity in realization does not arise exclusively in relation to personal will. There are other qualities that call forth the sense of solidity, such as truth, existence, universal will, and impeccability to mention a few. But our first encounter with a presence of solidity is often with will as silver. The Six's ego ideal attempts to mimic true will by finding an emotional and mental solidity in order to feel secure, grounded, unswayed, and steadfast. But the Six can only accomplish this with an inflexible hardness that is defensive and insensitive to situations and people. Iron will can be considered a kind of will; however, it is a reflection of real will. It is defensive and hard phenomenologically but also emotionally. It appears as willfulness or stubbornness, as intransigence in opinions and understanding and in pushing through without consideration of consequences to others or the environment. While personal will is an expression of openness, the false or iron will shows no openness to people or circumstances. Difference only means opposition to the fixated Six—it is not something to be welcomed—and hence counter-phobic Sixes always challenge what is different, while phobic Sixes may submit to it with compliance.

The presence of solidity impacts our consciousness by making us feel secure and safe, grounded and supported. The Six's sense of fear is related to the absence of this presence. When we do not have our inner solidity, the feeling is of castration: a loss of will and its power. It is an intense (though often unconscious) sense of being cut off from our ground. The response to this in-tolerable castration—the palpable absence of inner solidity—is insecurity, fear, and anxiety, which are the central characteristics of the phobic Six. The fear response in counterphobic Sixes is covered over by hardness and rigidity compensating for the missing solidity. This inflexibility is what reveals the false will as fake, for true will is flexible even when firm. It is unflap-pable in the face of challenge or threat and responsive in the face of truth and reality. Hence the liberated individual flows with situations as they arise and responds intelligently and with flexibility in dealing with those situations. There is no sense of weakness associated with being flexible, while for the fixated Six, flexibility implies weakness.

The inner solidity that feels miraculously like compact, dense consciousness allows us to perceive our true grounding in reality and, hence, makes us less vulnerable to the sway of projections or imagined fears. It gives us a sense of true support, making us feel sustained by our own inner resources. We don't need external support most of the time to be who and what we are and to express ourselves and our ideas and feelings. There is no fear because the inner support and solidity gives us an authentic sense of safety and security.

Actually, the feeling of security comes when the personal will aspect fills the first chakra, the Muladhara, which is the center of self-preservation and survival located in the pelvic region (*mula* means "root" and *adhara* means "support"). When obstacles block the arising of will in this center, we feel insecure and tend to be fearful, even paranoid. Our survival does not feel certain because the center of security is lacking the essential quality of will that makes us feel secure in ourselves. When personal will is present in this first chakra, our perception of the environment in terms of threat or danger is objective and not derived from our projections, fantasies, or previous experiences.

It is common knowledge that we need will to persevere. But the way the fixated type approximates the necessary will is by pushing and trying and at other times by hardening oneself and one's sensitivity. With true will, the perseverance is natural and effortless. In fact, effortlessness is one of the effects of the presence of personal will. And we cannot know true effortlessness, which is important in many spiritual practices, without embodying personal will. True will imparts the distinct sense of confidence both in ourselves and in reality. Confidence is actually the presence of the quality of will in our consciousness, most of the time appearing in the solar plexus.

Perseverance becomes determination, which in turn can become effortless persistence. It appears from the outside as if one is applying one's will. But it is not an application; the will is simply present. Perseverance and persistence are the outer manifestations of the condition of steadfastness, which is a feeling that arises when we are being impacted by true will. Confidence breeds steadfastness, which is effortless because we are flowing with the truth. True confidence and steadfastness contrast with the stuttering and indecisiveness of the phobic Six or the stubbornness of the counterphobic Six, both indicating the lack of access to personal will.

In the previous chapter we explored the aspect of strength. Here we can see how strength will also be of help if it is present with will. True strength gives us the feeling of capacity, of "I can," and that will help us feel the steadfastness of "I will." Where strength provides the energy to initiate action, the will enables us to carry that action to fruition.

The steadfastness or persistence can also manifest as resoluteness and at some point as a true dedicated commitment. In fact, we cannot truly commit to a course of action or to a relationship if we do not have our own personal will, because without it we are uncertain and suspicious, insecure and untrusting of ourselves. We doubt our perceptions and insights and engage in imaginary threats and projections of outside dangers. A good example of this from literature is the character of Don Quixote created by Cervantes. This does not mean having true will eradicates external dangers but that we see them and assess them realistically rather than from fear or paranoia. We will be solid and confident even if our life is threatened. Because will provides the capacity for commitment, we are steady in our course of action; we do not sway and vacillate in our relationship to individuals, organizations, or causes.

The grounding of will, which brings a freedom from fantasy and projections, facilitates clarity and objectivity in all situations and relationships. Our resulting behavior is secure and unhesitating, concrete and certain. We experience a definiteness in our perception, observations, and understanding, for will supports us in seeing the truth as it is, free of fear or imagination.

In conventional knowledge, it seems paradoxical to think of will as effortless. Most people think will has to do with effort, that we need to apply our will and try hard to persist. But in fact, effortlessness is a by-product of the presence of personal will. For awakened beings, persistence and steadfastness require no effort; they come naturally and easily. And this can be a way that faith expresses itself. The solidity of will underlies faithfulness. This is actually counter to the understanding of will in conventional wisdom.

The more we understand will by embodying it, the more we see that persistence, determination, and resoluteness are all approximations of true will. They are good approximations, but approximations nevertheless. There is no striving in true will. If there were, then it would follow that divine will must also involve effort. When creating the world, does God strive and try and persist? Isn't it more likely that spontaneous effortless creation just happens? Something similar to that is the experience of the Six type once liberated from their fixation.

It is not easy to divine the aspect by simply knowing the ego ideal, because the ideal is only a reflection of will. Until we know the presence of will, we do not have a full and true understanding of what personal will is in reality. It is possible, but not easy, to figure it out. However, there is a more direct way to arrive at this knowing.

THE DIRECT APPROACH TO WILL

The tantric approach for this type would be to work with fear directly, which is obviously not so easy. Engaging spiritual practice consistently over time can support developing the capacity to stay with the fear and not run from it. We can eventually even welcome it. As we can feel fear completely, without identification, acting out, or avoidance, we start understanding it simply as energy, a kind of excitation. As we stay with this type of energy, we discover it is actually nothing but awareness, the clarity of awareness. Fear makes us alert. Biologically it acts as the catalyst for alertness in both animals and humans. Alertness is a more focused awareness than we might normally experience. It is awareness coming through our self-preservation instinct, which here is distorted through the neurosis that develops for the type. However, as we learn to make friends with fear, it reveals its source as clear, sharp awareness. It is not the aspect of personal will, which is the idealized quality, but it is the ground for it.

Since we need the idealized quality as the key to unlocking the fixation, how do we access the quality? What supports opening to its arising? Though it can lead to clear crisp awareness, the tantric method does not work for will. We cannot move to true will by just feeling the iron—or false—will, or by more intensely sensing our efforting. This just magnifies the false will. However, we can explore the state of iron will: our stubbornness and inflexibility, our effortful determination and persistence. Or we can explore the state of no will: our fearfulness and lack of confidence, our indecisiveness and hesitation, our doubt and insecurity. Exploring means to feel them as they are and not try to change them. It means to feel them and be open to understanding whatever meaning they might hold or might hide. To be curious about what it means to have an iron will, i.e., to be so incredibly stubborn regardless of how it annoys our friends and loved ones. We can inquire with curiosity and inquisitiveness into any of the iron will's traits without rejecting them, judging them, or trying to change or suppress them. If we feel fear or paranoia, we acknowledge the feelings without listening to the stories we tell ourselves about them. We should always assume we do not understand them completely, that there is still something about any of the feelings that remains to be discovered.

This kind of inquiry leads us first to what we idealize, how we want to be. This can in turn take us to the lack of what we want, the lack of feeling personal will: our lack of true confidence and the incapacity for real steadfastness. As we tolerate this lack and are patient with it, not assuming it is the end of the story, it will begin to reveal our disconnection from will, which can feel like a kind of castration. We might feel a lack of solidity, of confidence, and of security. Experiencing this state of lack can bring up the history of disconnection from personal will: things that happened early on in our life, when we naturally had will and confidence but lost them. This can illuminate what happened to disconnect us. Were we castrated by a person or an event? Were we constantly put down and not trusted? Was our confident groundedness not appreciated? This process can uncover many wounds. It is important to feel them and fully understand them experientially. This means we experience all the emotions that these memories and associations bring up, embracing them and being curious about them instead of locking them in the dungeon of our unconscious. Deviance and delinquency, the traits used to describe the Six in the Enneagram of avoidances, do not seem to clearly reflect the truth of this disconnection. The avoidance for each fixation refers to the deficient way the person experiences the loss of connection with essence. Deviance and delinquency can be due to a disconnection from will, but I have not personally observed them much in Six types.

As we remain with the lack of will and understand the circumstances that cut us off from it, the lack shows itself as a particular state of deficiency. This deficiency generally manifests as an emptiness, an empty hole in the solar plexus or an emptiness in the belly indicating a castrated or absent will. Yet, staying present with a curious mind and having the courage to be with the direct experience of the deficient emptiness will tend to dissolve the sense of deficiency and reveal the emptiness as a clear spaciousness. From within that spacious emptiness—which is transparent and clean, without any ideas or beliefs or expectations of what might happen next—the presence of personal will can emerge and fill us from inside. It might descend into us or well up inside us. The point is that the true will arises now that the obstacles preventing it have been cleared.

It can be the full moon of will, the white light presence of will, or the metallic silver of will, whether solid or liquid. It can arise in the solar plexus or in the belly or fill the whole body. As it arises, we feel erect and tall, present and solid, secure and confident, and definite in knowing we are embodying our authentic being. If we are a Six, we now have the key to unraveling our fixation and tackling its core with more capacity. It is the appropriate tool from the invisible world, and it helps us liberate ourselves from all the distorting, crippling, and problematic patterns and traits. At the same time, we are regaining access to an important aspect of our being that will help us in living our life with confidence and steadfastness, just as it can assist us in our practices with true commitment and certainty. We can focus and stay steady in that focus. We can be mindful and not forget the mindfulness thanks to our natural steadfastness and a genuine, nonconceptual commitment.

4

Point Two
MERGING LOVE

Point Two, which Ichazo called Ego-Flat and is also called the Helper, brings us to a different terrain on both the personality and essential levels. Twos flatter to get what they want, which is love and connection, especially connection to an idealized figure in whose shadow this type feels he or she can get the love, attention, specialness, worth, and support they feel they lack. Twos idealize helpfulness and related traits that compose a whole picture of an ideal. When they are healthy and free of the knots of the fixation, the helpfulness is genuine, heartful giving. We see that on the Enneagram of idealizations the phrases relevant for type Two are "helpfulness" and "giving." The helpfulness is an expression of true loving connection. However, the fixated type gives in order to get. It is a kind of manipulation. They can be codependent this way, but unconsciously they crave their independence and autonomy. Their insecurity, coupled with their need for specialness, manifests in a distinct sense of pride that is obvious to others in social situations. Relationships are central in their lives and the focus of most of their libidinal and emotional energy.

In *The Spiritual Dimension of the Enneagram*, Sandra Maitri writes the following about this type:

> Ingratiating themselves and being helpful, they try to make themselves indispensable. Rather than ask directly for what they want from others—especially affection—they give it and tokens of it with the expectation that the other will reciprocate. Hidden strings are thus attached to all of Two's giving—and Twos can be extremely generous with their time, resources, and even their bodies.... Presenting themselves with a veneer of false humility, beneath the surface Twos suffer from a prideful self-inflation, feeling themselves to be special, like Fours, entitled to singular treatment.[1]

THE IDEALIZED ASPECT: MERGING LOVE

It is easy to see how the various traits and behaviors listed above—and many others that characterize the shell of this type—are all attempts to regain or actualize a kind of essential love and, most significantly, how the basis of the ego ideal is to approximate and imitate some of this essential love's characteristics. It is very important for us to realize that conventionally we do not truly understand love, only some of its characteristics. Further, even those characteristics tend to be self-serving and, hence, distorted. For our present study it's important to recognize that there is not just one love but many kinds of love and that the word *love* encompasses approximations of several distinct essential qualities of love. Twos tend to idealize and desire not just any form of love, but one specific kind of love: the love that embodies the principle of connection, of feeling intimately connected through increasing degrees of intimacy, all the way to total merging and oneness. Of course, Twos actually want and need all of the kinds of love, but what they idealize is the particular way our spiritual nature expresses its love. All kinds of love are important in relationships and are expressed mostly in that context. But this particular love is central for relationships because it is the glue that makes them real relationships.

Many of us vaguely remember this kind of love from our very early life. It is a primary quality that pervades the good mother-child relationship in the first few months, and even the first year, of infancy. It is the basis of healthy attachment, for it is true connection. Most of us seek it later in our relationships, especially in our intimate love relationships. But others of us avoid it depending on the dynamics we experienced in our early relationship with our mother (or mothering person). Or we can be ambivalent about it, tending to experience unsureness and difficulty in sustaining a healthy relationship or marriage.

This kind of love is not simply an appreciation for or liking of another, which actually points to a different essential quality of love. It is not passionate ecstatic love either, for this again points to a third quality of love.[2] All are important for relationships but most relevant for us here is the merging love, which literally forms the relationship, provides the essence of genuine connection, and helps the relationship endure beyond a mere encounter.

However, to feel this love with another makes us vulnerable because we experience our heart as melted and surrendered. We feel intimately connected to the other in a kind of ecstatic oneness that is both sweet and nourishing. When we have this love we feel nourishment, connection, sweetness, and pleasure, and we no longer know where one begins and the other ends. There is a fulfilling sense of being one—inseparable, supported, and enriched.

PRESENCE OF MERGING LOVE

The direct experience of the presence of this love is uncommon and difficult to come by. Even for those who experience it, it is occasional and fleeting and depends on our circumstances. It is the heart in a true way, a way necessary for all the heart-centered, or *bhakti*, paths because it is needed for connecting to the divine, for becoming one with the divine. In our work, we refer to it as merging gold for very important reasons. Many people think of love as golden, but only this love is truly golden.

The feeling of this love in the heart is a kind of sweetness that does not have an earthly counterpart. There is no sweetness I know that is similar to this particular taste of sweetness. Other qualities of love possess a sweetness that we can recognize from tastes of things we know in our life, but not this kind of love. Love is frequently disarming, but here it is more than disarming; it is also melting. We can feel as if our heart is melting into love. But the melting is actual, not metaphorical. The heart or the nature of the heart feels melted in the way butter melts. We feel an actual, almost physical sensation of melting and flowing. The nature of this love is a substantial presence that melts our heart and mind gently and in sweetness. It melts whatever part of our inner subjectivity it touches. It might even feel as if it is melting our body. But this is a subjective feeling, for the body is only becoming deeply relaxed, at ease, and open. The sensation, however, is of melting—so we can accurately call this melting love. Yet I refer to it as *merging* love. The effect on two people, or one person in relation to nature or the divine, is a sense that one melts into the other, merges with the other, and feels one with the other, even though there is some awareness of differentiation. It's as if our consciousness or our sense of our being merges with the other, whether human or divine. We can feel melted from the inside, or melted together. We might feel merged from the inside outward, or merged in the sense of being taken in and melted by the other.

Most experience merging love as an arising in their consciousness, usually centered in the heart but sometimes flowing to different parts of the body or even filling it. The experience of melting feels like the body's boundaries dissolve and there is no sense of separateness from the other. This is why we use the word *merging*, for it is the merging of the two: self and other. As in infancy, the merging does not completely eliminate our sense of being who we are. But the connection is so complete and overwhelming that the boundaries between the two become porous and melt. In addition to melting sweetness, the affect is also an unusual and fulfilling kind of pleasure—rich, very distinct, and ecstatic. It feels as though our soul is being nourished by a divine, or heavenly, kind of pleasure.

The pleasure and ecstasy of this love is further enhanced by a visual glimpse of its presence. What we see is a beautiful, pure, transparent golden fluid. Hence the name merging gold. It is golden in a way that is different from gold metal, gold light, or gold color. This fluid is like honey, but it is not as dense or sticky as honey. It flows more easily and effortlessly, having less viscosity. There is a brightness and inherent luminosity to this golden fluid as if sunlight is passing through it, warm, sweet, and radiant. It is such a beauty to behold and such an ecstatic pleasure to sense or feel this kind of love.

However, it is not an emotion or a physical liquid. It is an essential presence that, most of the time, has a fluid sense to it with either a feeling of flow or of pooling. When two people experience merging gold together in a complete way, they feel that they form a sweet and luminously golden pool of pleasurable love. A whole group can feel it together, which happens in some of our teaching groups when everybody perceives themselves part of the sweet pool, or that the room is raining sweet golden love. There is no sense of wanting or possessiveness in it. Instead, the sense is of letting go or surrendering our heart. However, the most important feeling in this state is of presence, of a medium or expanse with its own weight and substance, a substance that is the fullness of existing, the fullness of being, and of being present here and now. We can feel the pooling love as the presence that is here, or we can feel our own presence because of this merging presence in our consciousness. Either way we feel more ourselves, with our hearts open and melted in pleasure and enjoyment.

The presence can have different densities—at times light like vapor, at other times dense like a substantial presence. When it is light, on the lataif level of inner experience, it seems to fill the air with a delicate, weightless fluidity that is transparent, luminous gold. Even the full presence has degrees of density, depending on how fully and deeply we experience it, or how it presents itself. For instance, our being can present the aspect of merging gold as a flowing stream with the density of water. However, the loving consciousness can become denser, more concentrated, giving it a sense of more fullness, more depth, and more richness. In whatever way it manifests, merging gold can be localized in the heart or the whole chest, or it can flow throughout the whole body and even ooze out of it. We can feel it pervading everything, melting the boundaries of whatever it touches.

So heart is actual presence, not just feeling and affect. There is an affect of love, which is a pleasurable sweetness and the enjoyment of the other, and yet love itself is a presence, a medium, a mass that has expanse. And this medium of merging gold is always transparent, whether it is light or dense. It is not opaque, like silver. It is a clear, sweet golden medium or continuum that has the sense of immediacy similar to all other qualities of Being. It gives us the feeling that we are present in the here and now, for it is the presence of now.

CHARACTERISTICS OF MERGING LOVE

Understanding the ego ideal of type Two can largely explain their traits and behavioral tendencies. Of course, the core of the fixation and the Two's specific life history also exert their own influence. Here we are finding the key to working with all the influences, which is the key hidden in the ego ideal of the type. By seeing how the ego ideal is an approximation of the idealized aspect, we understand more fully the shell of the fixation and also gain access to the key for the type.

The Two's overriding interest and investment in relationships—in having the ideal intimate relationship with somebody important—is a direct reflection of the need for the merging gold kind of love. When we do not have access to this quality of our essential nature, being in an intimate relationship comes close to replicating how it feels. But it is really not that close. The merging gold love is the essence of connection; when we experience it we know we are not separate. So it is at the heart of what a relationship is, and the more it is present in a relationship the closer and more satisfying it feels. Most intimate relationships derive some satisfaction from a kind of closeness and connection that is a mere reflection of the connection of merging gold. Without this sense of connection there is aloneness and loneliness, which can be painful and make our life feel empty.

The Two craves all kinds of connection in relationships, including those with friends and family and groups and organizations but especially in an intimate relationship. This is definitely primary for the sexual type, but important for the other instinctual types as well. Of course, relationships are important for all human beings, but this type has a more pronounced investment in them, which we can see in the other traits. For example, Twos generally have a difficult time in relationships precisely because of their unconscious need for merging love. Some are challenged to even find a sustainable relationship, and of those who do, many end up getting stuck in a situation of dependency.

Because of their lack of access to merging gold, and the history with parental figures around this lack, Twos usually end up being quite dependent inside, regardless of how independent they appear. This manifests in codependency, in which they take on the role of the giver, even though it's clear the giving is not selfless and pure. As givers they idealize helping, but the help has an agenda: to feel helped. It is codependent because the individual covers up their dependency by helping others and creating the impression that others depend on them. It is a well-known pattern that cannot be completely resolved without some depth of integration of the merging gold love. This will require letting go of the identity that is dependent on a kind of support derived from feeling connected and merged with another.

This is the reason why Twos tend to idealize some figure, an authority or a famous person. They extend affection and help of many kinds to that person in order to establish a connection. Even without marriage or intimate relationship, just feeling connected and important to this figure provides some satisfaction, some sense of protection, nourishment, and support. They enjoy basking in the glow of the idealized figure, for it makes them feel both special and connected.

Twos nourish others because they themselves need nourishment, which is again an expression of the codependent position they often take. Yet the true nourishment they seek exists in the actual state of merging gold and its sense of rich, sweet presence. They go to great lengths to get the effects of this state in the form of nourishment, connection, safety, and support, using manipulation as their principal tool. That manipulation then spreads to other areas of their lives, becoming a basic strategy to get anything they want or need. One of these manipulative tactics, especially in relationship to idealized figures, is outright flattery. Flattery is actually a primitive tool of manipulation that only works on people who need it. Not surprisingly, Twos often end up in relationships with individuals who are needy like themselves.

Why choose manipulation? The answer lies in the fact that the primary position Twos take, that of codependency, is itself a hidden manipulation. The more fixated the Two type, the more manipulative they are in relationship to others. This means Twos deploy a spectrum of manipulative tendencies to get the desired nourishment, from the most obvious and primitive to the very subtle and indirect, which can be hard for the inexperienced eye to detect. They themselves might not be aware of their manipulations, but friends, colleagues, and partners will often feel manipulated without knowing why. This causes most of the fallings-out in the social sphere of Twos' relationships.

Twos can share themselves generously. For healthy Twos it is a real sharing, but for fixated Twos with various degrees of fixation the sharing is selective, and friends frequently end up feeling betrayed or disappointed, for these Twos still keep much concealed. When merging gold is integrated, the sharing, especially social sharing, is fundamental to it. However, when this love is the source, there is no holding back, no boundaries, no hiddenness, and no manipulation. The liberated Two excels at this authentic and open sharing. They can be powerful community builders, where many can enjoy the results of this sharing and connection.

Regardless of their codependent façade, type Twos crave independence and autonomy. This becomes obvious the more they become liberated from the constraining patterns of the shell. But even then, their move toward independence will often include manipulation, hidden agendas, and strings attached, for manipulation is a specific reaction in the inner core of their fixation. A great deal of deep work is required to resolve this reaction. Having access to the real connectedness of the merging essence can be a key that penetrates the core. It gives them a kind of autonomy because they already have the merging and do not need to look for it elsewhere. It also gives their intelligence the kind of independence and freedom needed to work with the core.

THE DIRECT APPROACH
TO MERGING LOVE

The best way for Twos to access the idealized aspect reflected in the ego ideal is to specifically investigate their disproportionate investment in relationships. This includes looking at their codependent position to reveal the inner dependency and need for a nourishing connection. Most of Twos' traits point to this need for connection; their underlying dependency reflects the absence of connection. By becoming aware that they are lacking the connection they always seek—which can appear as pursuing specialness in a community or group—they come close to disconnection from the essential quality. Disconnection from merging gold is not easy to tolerate, and

Twos end up feeling bereft and lonely, abjectly indigent, and sometimes even abandoned and forgotten. The qualities of strength and will can be helpful here. They make it easier to stay with this lack and to feel the disconnection.

Feeling the loneliness, emptiness, and impoverishment that go with the disconnection is the most direct way we can reconnect with the merging love. But first we need to experience and be comfortable with feeling not connected and not having the love and pleasurable nourishment that our soul needs. We must be aware of our manipulation, especially the way it happens in codependency. When we arrive at this point in our inner experience, it is easy for the disconnection to reveal itself as an emptiness that has loneliness and a lack of love and richness. Frequently Twos experience this deficiency as neediness, as the Enneagram of avoidances indicates. There is the distinct sense of neediness for loving connection that can appear as an emptiness in the lower part of the chest, for the center of merging essence is at the left side of the sternum.

Naranjo, whose book views the types in terms of their particular passions and how they are a consequence of disconnection from being, writes the following of this type:

> We may say that, despite superficial elation, vitality and flamboyance, there lurks in proud character a secret recognition of emptiness—a recognition transformed into the pain of hysterical symptoms, into eroticism and clinging to love relationships.[3]

Going through the deficient emptiness is a kind of partial ego death and leads to an opening, a spaciousness that can open the center of this aspect, like taking a cork out of a bottle or untying a knot. This allows the river of inner goodness to flow and nourish the impoverished soul, maybe for the first time ever. The reward for tolerating this lonely and impoverished emptiness is then the upwelling of the beautiful transparent flowing golden love. It is like a bubbling in the lower part of the chest or a fountain in the heart. Our heart seems to exude this nourishing sweetness. We feel uplifted by this exquisite quality and its amazing sweetness, which not only satisfies and fulfills but also melts our hearts and edges and relaxes us into a sense of primordial safety. We feel that all we need is here.

In this way, if we are a Two, we have resolved and clarified the patterns of our type that constrain our soul and deprive her of freedom. Now we also have access to a tool that helps us approach the deeper core, penetrate it, and melt it. Besides unraveling the deeper knots of the type and supporting our inner practice, the experience and integration of this aspect is quite an addition to our life. As an enormous enrichment of our heart, the merging love can spill over to our relationships and life in general. Our giving becomes genuine, the heart connectedness is real, and flattery and manipulation are no longer needed. In other words, the integration of the merging gold into one's soul makes type Two more sincere and truthful, more direct and transparent in their interactions and dealings with the world. These are some of the expressions of the liberated Two. But you don't have to be a Two to have this generous heartfulness or this way of approaching life and relationships. You simply need access to the essential quality.

5

Point One
BRILLIANCY

Point One, or Ichazo's Ego-Resent (also called the Reformer), idealizes perfection, rightness, goodness, improvement, and other related traits, and these qualities form its ego ideal. Naranjo writes, "The main activity that promises abundance to the ennea-type one mind is the enactment of perfection."[1] But there are many things that result from perfection and rightness as an ego ideal. The Enneagram of idealizations describes this idea as "I am right" and "I am good." We can understand much of the shell of the fixation for this type through this ideal, and we can understand even more by knowing the idealized quality and its characteristics.

Ones believe they are good, and they want that good for others and, hence, to improve things and make them better, more perfect. This desire is sincere when Ones are free from the constraints and the limiting patterns of their fixation. Many Ones throughout history have done a lot of good this way, notably the ancient Chinese philosopher Confucius. But when they are not free from the ego ideal, it can become a rigid and fixed movement toward a standard of perfection and goodness that comes from Ones' mind, from the patterning of their early experience, and from the distortions they have of the true quality related to this ideal. They might have a feeling or intuition that things can be right, but they can't help but distort this rightness through the lens of their superego. Hence, they can become critical both of themselves and others. They can become judgmental and resentful, trying hard to reform themselves, others, or situations according to the standards of their superego. A clear example is the case of the many missionaries who traveled to distant lands to convert the indigenous population into perfect Christians, not according to Christ's teachings but according to their internalized standards of perfection.

As Freud taught, the ego ideal is part of the structure of the superego, and there is no clearer case of this than type One. The superego judges according to its ego ideal. It can be harsh, judgmental, critical, and stern, partly due to the One's distortions of the idealized aspect and partly due to the internalized superegos of their parents or even cultural or religious influences. The more harsh and judgmental the parents were with type One, the more this type will end up being harsh and judgmental in their perfectionistic attempts to change and reform people and things. Here's how Hudson and Riso describe it in *The Wisdom of the Enneagram*:

> Ones believe that being strict with themselves (and eventually becoming "perfect") will justify themselves in their own eyes and in the eyes of others. But by attempting to create their own brand of perfection, they often create their own personal hell. . . . When Ones have gotten completely entranced in their personality, there is little distinction between them and this severe, unforgiving voice. Separating from it and seeing its genuine strengths and limitations is what growth for Ones is about.[2]

Freud believed that the superego and its ideals form our conscience. And so it is the place where our morality comes from. But this is the conscience of the ego, which has no true source for knowing what a real conscience is. Rather, it is borrowed from what we encounter in our lives, especially from what the important people in our childhood considered a true and moral compass. The ego, or the fixated soul, has no idea that our essential being has the principles of true conscience and that that conscience can guide us with the true morality of being, which is flexible and responsive, never rigid or harsh, inhumane or cruel.

THE IDEALIZED ASPECT: BRILLIANCY

Point Ones can look wholesome and bright-eyed. This actually reflects the idealized quality of essential intelligence, and we will understand why as we study it. Most people think that intelligence has to do with our IQ, with our brain, or with how many synapses or how much gray matter we have. Or we believe we are born with a certain degree of intelligence, which is mental and has to do with being clever, bright, or brilliant in our ideas, thoughts, theories, or proposals. We sometimes call smart people brilliant. But what does brilliance have to do with intelligence? Do these intelligent people shine and radiate light? Did Einstein illuminate a dark room when he entered it? Of course not, but this notion points to a deep intuition about real intelligence that explains the metaphor of brilliance. Real intelligence turns out to be a quality of being that shines with an intense brightness, which led us to call this aspect brilliancy.

Brilliancy differs from the other aspects we have been working with in an important way that gives it many of its characteristics. Each essential quality or aspect is unique and different from other aspects; it explicitly manifests a quality that is implicit in our being. So our true being, our true self—or our spiritual nature—has implicit within it will, strength, joy, merging gold, and so on. The essence of intelligence is different from all of these in that it manifests all the qualities of Being in one quality. This quality has in it all other qualities, but they are synthesized completely and without differentiation within it. They function as one quality. So brilliancy expresses all qualities while it appears as a single quality, that of essential intelligence. This means that intelligence includes all aspects of being in its presence and utilizes their totality in its functioning.

Hence one associated characteristic is that of completeness. It is this completeness that gives it the affect, or sense, of perfection. Brilliancy is perfect because it is complete; it includes all of Being's sublime qualities. We feel complete when we experience this aspect, not just intelligent. This means that intelligence on the essential level is a complete manifestation of true nature, but it appears in our individual consciousness as a particular unique quality with its own texture, feel, density, viscosity, and color. Even though brilliancy is the aspect of intelligence, it is not limited to the head. It does appear in the head when we are using our mind in an insightful or wise way, but it also appears in the heart when we are responding emotionally and utilizing our heart capacities in an intelligent way. It can also infuse the belly when our actions and movements are graceful, effective, and to the point.

We learn something important about intelligence in all of this: Intelligence has to do with completeness, with using all of our spiritual qualities in a synthesized way. The resulting functioning has the sense of being totally right; so right that it is perfect. And perfection has to do with completeness of being, of having no gap in being ourselves.

PRESENCE OF BRILLIANCY

As with the other qualities, there are many ways brilliancy manifests in various degrees of density and fullness in our experience. The texture is quite striking when we first experience it. It feels smooth—so fluid and perfect in its smoothness that it seems logical that it could penetrate our neurons and all our little hidden corners. Because it is so smooth, it flows anywhere gently and without resistance and seems to have no viscosity. It does not need to push in order to penetrate, because its smoothness makes it fine enough to seep into cracks and permeate surfaces.

Similar to but lighter than the consistency of mercury, while still being dense and substantial, brilliancy can manifest in a powerful, immense way. I remember the first time intelligence explicitly manifested in my individual consciousness. My body was shaking and quaking. I did not know what was happening, but I was feeling something strong going on in the middle of my chest at the sternum. Something was erupting with intensity and power. As it pushed through whatever was obstructing it, the feeling was of immensity—an immense presence, powerful and dense. As the presence with its immense potency came through me, it felt intense, huge and forceful, and it impacted everybody else in the room. Eventually the shaking subsided enough for me to perceive its smoothness, the exquisiteness of its fluidity.

One thing I learned from this experience is that the center of brilliancy is not in the head but located right at the center of the body, at the middle of the lower end of the sternum. You may recall that the merging essence emerges from the left side of this center that we call the mobius. It is not one of the lataif or one of the chakras but a secret center related to a subtle network of centers that I have not heard of or read about anywhere. This is a deeper network than the chakra and lataif systems. The network is not all about intelligence, but the mobius is, as the essence of intelligence emerges from the middle of the mobius.

The exploding emergence of the quality was the beginning. After that, brilliancy mostly appeared as a smooth, dense, amazingly brilliant-looking fluid whose smoothness made it incredibly responsive, with no viscosity or stickiness and a completely frictionless flow. The sleek texture by itself is delightful and pleasurable in the way that one naturally enjoys exquisite refinement. But this aspect is not just about affect. It can flow anywhere in the body or head, appearing frequently in the brain as the intellect becomes active on the essential level. It gives the mind the capacity to synthesize—to see the underlying thread that unifies many separate things—because it is the prototype of synthesis. And synthesis is one of the qualities of true intelligence, reflecting the fact that it is a synthesis of all essential qualities. When it is operating in the brain or head, the effect is close to what people refer to as being brilliant, for it can allow our mind to function brilliantly. The presence can also appear as a pooling of smooth, dense fluid in the belly, making us feel full of presence, or present in a full dense manner. We can feel delicate and refined while being dense and immense in our presence. It is an exquisite way of experiencing and knowing presence.

What is most striking about brilliancy is that it has no color, and that is because it has all colors. Just like sunlight has no color but includes the whole spectrum of colors. Yet even this does not accurately describe the visual experience, which is more like looking at the sun directly or seeing the shine of sunlight reflecting off water. What we see is the color of brilliance—so bright and intense that it is hard to look at it. However, because it is the intense luminosity of our spiritual nature, we can look directly at it without hurting our inner eye. Here we are not talking about intelligence in terms of its effect or functioning; we are talking about how its presence looks. The essence of intelligence is pure brilliance and rather than an intensified characteristic of a given color or light (such as brilliant white), brilliance, in the essential presence of brilliancy, has become an experience in itself. That is why there is nothing like it on earth, on the physical plane.

The nature of brilliancy is the pure brilliance of light, compact and dense. It is the luminosity of light in its intensity.[3] And the presence is brilliance through and through, not just on the surface. Brilliance as a substantial medium or a field of presence. It is not transparent, for the whole field of brilliance radiates brightness. It is an amazing truth that there is such a thing, such a reality.

Invariably we recognize the presence of brilliancy as intelligence. Many people when they first experience this essential quality in themselves use the word *intelligence*. When someone is remarkably dazzling in their intelligence, I think we would find a few drops of brilliancy in their brain or in the medium of their consciousness. And the way it affects our state is that we actually feel brilliant—we feel bright and penetrating and effective. So, the look of brilliancy translates into the brilliance of intelligent functioning. We use words like *brilliant* and *bright* because we intuitively know that intelligence has the subtle visual characteristic of intense brightness. Intelligence is made of the brilliance of Being, which is the true radiance of Being, our essential presence. I think this is one reason that people who behold the presence of spiritual light often say it is white or brilliant white. It is whiteness that is so bright that the white disappears in the brilliance.

Point One: Brilliancy 73

CHARACTERISTICS OF BRILLIANCY

Now we can see what the ego ideal is trying to emulate. Brilliancy, or essential intelligence, has the affect of completeness, of no gap, of nothing missing. Hence it feels like perfection. Since it expresses our being in all of its sublime qualities, it is pure perfection. This is an instance of the connection between the holy idea—holy perfection, for the One—and the essential endowment; brilliancy with its inherent perfection. The perfection is not in something external or in an action or creation; nor is it based on a standard. The perfection is in the presence itself, which is completeness and also preciousness. So its affect includes all of these: completeness, rightness in all ways, perfection, preciousness, and innocence. From these affects come the traits of this type. Since Ones want to express the preciousness of true nature but don't actually know it, they want things and people, including themselves, to be complete, right, and perfect. They feel that their moral principles come from their conscience because they strongly believe their conscience knows what makes everything precious—and potentially perfect. While in reality their sense of preciousness is a mere reflection of the preciousness of true nature.

Since their ideal is not brilliancy itself but a reflection or approximation of some of its characteristics, their ideal becomes perfection and rightness, goodness and improvement. Perfection is certainly a characteristic of brilliancy, but Ones think of it in terms of people's physical manifestations: thoughts, actions, and interactions, including their own and how they feel. They are perfectionistic, trying hard to always do the right thing as they mimic the action of brilliancy, which is always right on, to the point, effective, and complete. But what Ones think of as perfection has more to do with their ideas of perfection, which follow their assumptions and beliefs about how things should be and how people should behave, appear, feel, and act. Therefore, perfection does not express the intelligence of being but instead the ideas and judgments of the superego. And when Ones'—or others'—actions and opinions do not correspond to their standard of perfection, they become uncomfortable, resentful, righteous, and angry. They want things to be right, and they go to great lengths to set them right, according to standards they are certain are objective and should apply to everybody.

It is no wonder Ones can become reformers in their attempts to bring more rightness to the world, whether social, moral, political, ideological, philosophical, or otherwise. Awakened Ones do object to what is not right and not in harmony with Being and its perfection. But they are open-minded and flexible and responsive to people's states and stations. They care about the nuances of life, and they are not rigid or inflexible as fixated Ones are. Brilliancy is quite fluid and appears in awakened and liberated Ones as flexibility in their moral compass and as a recognition of people's limitations and capacities. They are intelligent in their attempt to reform and, hence, they are to the point. Their actions are not harsh judgments, resentful and angry punishments, or condemnations. Instead, they observe with intelligence what is going on and respond with complete action—that is, an action that takes into consideration the whole situation. We see this in the example of Mohammad, the prophet of Islam, who came first mostly as a reformer of the excesses and problems of his society. He was known to be an example of innocent rightness. However, this does not mean that every illuminated or liberated One is a reformer or activist. They each find their true calling. Brilliancy has no attitudes, opinions, or judgments; it is simply the presence of perfection as intelligence. So, we can express ourselves just right, meaning with the appropriate proportion of intensity or ease, gentleness or wrath, penetration or refinement. The point is true movement toward perfection, which is the realization of one's authentic being. Fundamentally, the right way is the path toward awakening and realization. The work is the Great Work, the inner work toward being what we are. Perfection is then natural, and we are right because we are upright in essential conscience, not uptight in a mentally constructed morality.

Ones believe they are good, try hard to be good, and frequently grew up as the good girl or boy. This is a reflection of the fact that brilliancy is all goodness, for it is the radiance of our true nature, what Plato termed "the Good." As the presence of brilliancy, we feel present in a full and perfect way, dense but fluid, intelligent and complete. We are the essence of goodness, with no fixed ideas or rigid views. Our intelligence and mind are fluid and flexible, with no rigidity or need to be unbending and unchangeable. Hence, our mind is open and pliant, making it not only intelligent but human and attuned. Ones tend to feel a strong need to be right. As the brilliant presence we don't need to be right; we can be wrong and when we are, we are willing to listen and learn. However, we are rightness itself, the rightness of true Being.

It's no wonder that Ones want to be good, for it is part of their ego ideal. But goodness for fixated Ones depends on a borrowed or constructed morality, which often means abrogating their responsibility to their true being. We can see the various traits of Ego-Resent as a reflection of a partial and distorted view of what the idealized aspect is. But we can use those traits to recognize what the ego ideal is, and if we can understand that the ego ideal is not real—that it is constructed and developed through the exigencies of time—we can see through it to get close to the idealized aspect.

Queen Elizabeth II is a One who has embodied a drive for perfection guided and constrained by royal traditions that provide unforgiving standards of behavior and appearance. However, as queen, she has not always been able to simply impose the standards of the past on her family or her country. Instead, she has had to understand the context and role of those standards. During her nearly seventy-year reign, Elizabeth has often been confronted by the tension between rigid tradition, effective functioning, and cultural necessity—a most poignant challenge for a One to face, and one that has undoubtedly moved her closer at times to an essential intelligence. The Queen is a good example of a One who has approximated the ideal in the right direction.

By not taking the ego ideal at face value but instead exploring it to see where it comes from, we will first encounter the influences in our life that formed our superego and our standards. We can discover where our judgments come from if we do not justify them to ourselves by blaming ourselves or others for having them. Becoming curious about the ego ideal and working to understand it can lead to the forgotten intuitions and feelings that form its nucleus. Seeing this nucleus may open the door to discovering where these feelings come from. In this process, we might open to brilliancy itself, the true perfection that gives our morality and conscience an essential ground.

THE DIRECT APPROACH
TO BRILLIANCY

A direct approach to brilliancy is to inquire into our ideas about the absence of perfection and rightness in our lives—why we always find wrongness and incorrectness and then get angry and resentful. We can look at the fact that we do not know perfection that is constant and incorruptible. This can lead to experiencing the disconnection from perfection and, in turn, to the deficient emptiness that opens the door to the true quality.

On the other hand, a more effective inquiry can be to explore our relationship to intelligence and find out if we feel we have it or we lack it. If we feel we have it, we want to find out what that intelligence is. If we feel we lack it, we want to understand this lack. Most people have to work on their relationship with their father in this process, for something about brilliancy impels us to project this quality onto our father—not in all situations but in most. To the soul, our father tends to represent brilliancy, just as mother represents merging gold. (Although this is true for the majority of people, there are certainly exceptions.) Brilliancy turns out to be the real father, just as merging gold is the true mother. They are the essential parents, representing the fact that as individual souls we are each an offspring of Being, our spiritual nature.

By integrating brilliancy—the essence of intelligence and the true perfection—we learn about our being in a significant way, and we know presence with more depth. Brilliancy is powerful for gaining synthesizing insights from many dimensions because it brings us a capacity for synthesis that is not available to the ordinary mind. And brilliancy also provides the specific key that can unravel the shell of the One type and help penetrate its deeper core.

6

Point Three
PERSONAL ESSENCE

Point Three—Ego-Go according to Ichazo's original parlance, the Achiever in others—is very concerned about image. But that image is based on a model of success that accords with the culture in which the Three lives. Threes are concerned with how people see them, and they value what they interpret as success and then work hard to achieve it. They are practical and effective in what they do, and they tend to get the job done. They are doers and accomplishers, and they possess abundant energy for achievement and excellence in whatever field they happen to choose. The Enneagram of idealizations describes the ego ideal for type Three as "I am successful" and "I can achieve."

But the more fixated they are, the more deceptive they are toward themselves and others, for truth tends to elude them. They value success as seen through the prism of their community over a deeper, truer sense of value. The image of success or fame—being the star who is valued by society—is their overriding concern, which results in total avoidance of the helplessness that characterizes their inner core.

Their specific reaction of striving appears as the ego ideal of efficiency. Threes are usually efficient but not at embodying their fundamental nature. Instead, they are efficient at creating the image of the idealized paradigm of society, as if this is what a human being ought to be. Naranjo writes, "In the service of efficiency, thinking tends to be precise and there is often a leaning towards mathematics. A fast tempo is also characteristic and has probably developed in the service of efficiency, as well as out of a desire to stand out through special efficiency."[1]

Sandra Maitri elaborates:

> They are driven and goal-oriented, and value success in the particular domain in which they are invested more than anything. Achieving what they set out to do takes precedence over every other concern, whether they be physical constraints, those of class or economic origin, or the feelings of others or even of themselves. They often drive themselves mercilessly in their pursuit of accomplishment, and may be perceived by others as ruthless, calculating and possessing a steely determination. Threes are pragmatic and matter-of-fact, doing whatever it takes to get the job done, including using manipulation and deception.[2]

The more fixated the type, the more deceptive, image-oriented, and ruthless they are about achieving their perceived status of excellence. Their idealization of efficiency, competence, and success tends to override the harmful consequences of their actions as they climb the ladder of success, frequently at the expense of others as well as their own integrity and truth. They seek worth and value, which tend to be external and seen through the eyes of what the culture idealizes instead of what is uniquely true about themselves. Hence, they are the most extroverted and dynamic of all the Enneatypes, and the most committed to putting in whatever effort is required to achieve their externally driven image of success. They appear to be personal and caring, but this personalness is often superficial and connected to some goal they want to achieve. It is an act, not truly felt, and performed without true understanding for or connection to who the other person truly is. The more liberated they are from the confines of the fixation the more truly personal they become, and their effectiveness is in the service of true functioning, not for image or for the eyes of others.

THE IDEALIZED ASPECT: PERSONAL ESSENCE

The personal essence might be one of the most unexpected and most misunderstood of all the essential qualities. Conventionally, people believe they know what it is like to be personal with somebody else and to make genuine contact with them. They also believe they know what a true human being is, what a person is. But in many cases, nothing could be further from the truth.

To understand what a human being is requires dedicated inner work and much maturation, which is why the few spiritual traditions that know this aspect refer to it as the "precious pearl" or "incomparable pearl." The hero of the spiritual quest ventures into the conventional world—the world of lies—to find the hidden pearl. In these traditions, the pearl is usually guarded by a fearsome dragon that symbolizes the overriding ego of the type. The hero must overcome or get past the dragon in order to retrieve the precious jewel and return with it to their spiritual home, which is now endowed with a quality that was not formerly available.

In other words, this quality—a personal beingness—is attained by wrestling with life's circumstances as the soul grows and matures until it becomes possible for it to individuate on the essential or spiritual level while living a human life. This realization contrasts with being a transcendent absolute or impersonal vastness and withdrawing from the world. The personal essence is an attainment, but unlike the outer accomplishment of the fixated Three, the attainment results from growing and developing, learning to be a human being who embodies our essential nature in our maturity. We are then both the transcendent and a real person, a person who expresses the transcendent by being a human being in the truest sense of the word.

From the Diamond Approach perspective, one of the assumptions that makes this aspect unexpected is the position—which people often accept as true because of what they hear in many spiritual teachings—that if one is a person, then one is bound to be ego. The belief is that only ego can be individual. Part of this fallacy is the position that an individual or person must be a separate entity and hence cannot be in the nondual condition, which means the individual is bound to be an illusion or construction. This position runs counter to the development in the Western world of valuing the individual—individual autonomy and uniqueness, individual human rights and contributions.

It is true that in its enshrining of the unique individual, Western culture is frequently enshrining the ego. But we have to wonder where the West got the idea that the individual with its personal uniqueness and variation is important in the first place. An even more important question is why do all human beings appear as individuals and live as such until they become aware of the vastness of the nondual, infinite, transcendent reality? Where did the soul learn to structure herself as an individual? Another observation that the nondual teachings tend to ignore is that no two realized nondual masters are the same, which points to the fact that individual difference is not incompatible with nondual equality.

It is also true that some human beings intuit a real individual as being one who is successful at being a true human person with true personalness and a capacity for relational contact and effective functionality, and one who makes human life meaningful instead of understanding it as an illusory stage on the way to the transcendent vastness. The idealization of type Three comes from this obscure intuition, but it is patterned by what one's society or group thinks of as an exemplary human individual. This erroneous ideal is compounded by the additional influence of one's particular personal history and one's encounters in life.

The ideal does not appear as the individual or person but as some associated characteristics of the essential quality: those of efficiency, competence, and excellence, especially in doing. Threes idealize efficiency and strive hard to be as proficient as possible. They try to be effective in their drive toward success and be competent in all that they do. They are focused on not wasting time, being down to earth and practical, and creating excellence to the best of their ability. But maintaining their image of efficiency and competence is important only for achieving what they believe will make them the human paragon of success in their society. Then they will have become what a human being "ought" to be, bringing with it acclaim, love, and admiration. Threes believe this will restore the lost love and attuned holding that will finally make it possible to simply relax and be, without a care in the world.

Hudson writes about the healthier example of this type:

Threes really can and do achieve great things in the world. They are the "stars" of human nature, and people often look up to them because of their graciousness and personal accomplishments. Healthy Threes know how good it feels to develop themselves and contribute their abilities to the world.... [They] embody the best in a culture, and others are able to see their hopes and dreams mirrored in them.... Threes act as living "role models" and paragons because of their extraordinary embodiment of socially valued qualities. Healthy Threes know that they are worth the effort it takes to be "the best that they can be."[3]

This is the example of the healthy type, and even though most Threes do not reach such exemplary development, it is still not the liberated type. The latter is the Three who has attained the key to their fixation, unraveled their shell, and penetrated its core. But we cannot understand this distinction without discussing what this aspect is and how it forms the ego ideal and the patterns of the shell.

PRESENCE OF PERSONAL ESSENCE

This presence is not known in or acknowledged by many teachings, although Taoism, the Sufi and Kabbalah teachings, and some areas of Christian mysticism do refer to it. The knowledge offered in this book has developed through the Diamond Approach teaching. It includes psychological knowledge developed in the twentieth century that was unavailable when these older teachings arose.[4] The personal essence, or pearl, arises as a form of presence, presence with form. It has a few stages of development because, unlike most other qualities of presence, it is intimately connected with a maturation of our soul, our individual consciousness, so that it embodies all the properties of cosmic consciousness.

I will relate three stages of its arising that come from my personal experience. These stages are relevant for our study here, but additional stages are important for nondual realization and other kinds of realization. The first stage for me was the development of a process in the heart, in the area of the physical heart. At one point I saw in this area what appeared to be a primitive crib in some kind of enclosure. There was a lot of merging gold present in the area of the heart and some whiteness in the crib. But the crib, made of gold, seemed to have an embryo in it, alive and quiet. It was like the soul had in it the beginning of a baby, as if it had been impregnated. Taoists speak of the divine embryo, but they see it developing in the belly, not in the heart.

The second stage was when my own process moved to the belly. The crib that seemed to be in a manger was one occurrence, and although I felt it as a process, it did not get my attention until it moved to the belly. Then, for some time, what I experienced was a fullness in the belly. The fullness over time got so big that I started feeling as if I were pregnant. The state lasted for a number of days, drawing my attention to it every so often. I knew it was some kind of presence but did not discern the quality yet. I felt full of presence and, at times, like presence itself. This feeling of fullness in the belly that makes some people feel pregnant is the most common experience for students before they recognize the personal essence directly and see its pearly form.

The third stage was the definitive experience, which happened sometime later while I was in a café. I used to frequent cafés in the 1980s, where I would write in my journal or talk with companions on the journey. I was contemplating and musing about an observation of myself. It was in the first few years after I had begun teaching students, and I was aware of being the presence that teaches, with openness and love and caring for everybody. Yet I had a subtle feeling of something missing in my teaching, especially in my relation to the students. I cared for all of them as a whole and individually as well, but I noticed that I was not as personal with them as I could be. It wasn't that I was *not* personal. I was personal in the conventional sense of the word, knowing them by name and interacting with each individually in an attuned and sensitive way. Nevertheless, something was missing. It was as though I was not being personal in a way that I still did not know.

Upon reaching this understanding in my inquiry, a deep dark hole opened up at the center of the chest. Out of this hole there popped an unexpected presence: a big pearl that became me. I felt myself as a round full pearl that felt fleshy in its fullness, resilient and flexible. It was a fullness that felt like a healthy young muscle, but it was not physical. The room felt as if it were bathed in an amber rain, which felt like the essence of value. I recognized that this presence, which was spontaneously born, had an unusual value for me, for the teaching and for humanity.

The main way the personal essence is experienced is as a rounded full presence; the sensation of fullness has the density and resilience of a hard-boiled egg. But it is not physical; it is all consciousness. (This aspect is seldom amorphous or indistinct, though it can be when needed—for instance when it becomes fluidlike, pervading the subjective atmosphere.) As this presence of fullness, the feeling is that one is presence that knows it is present and knows it is personal presence.

Personal here has two meanings. One is that it is capable of being personal in a more direct and simple way than is conventionally known. It is not personal as in telling stories about oneself or listening to other people's stories and personal situations. It just feels personal, as if it is the essence of being personal. It cannot be defined or broken down further. It is the essence of being personal that cannot be known except by experiencing this presence. I realized that the conventional sense of being personal that is expressed through words and actions is a reflection of this presence. This personalness is present just by being oneself with another person. We feel we are being personal without saying anything personal about ourselves. It is just how we are and how we interact. Furthermore, in the interaction, the uniqueness of the other is recognized and responded to—they feel that they are being contacted personally, that they are related to as another true person, as their own person, with all their qualities and capacities. The personal essence has this characteristic of being the essence of personalness.

Another meaning is that we feel we are a person, a real person. It turns out that this person is not reducible. "Person" is a Platonic idea or form, the prototype of the person, which is similar to being a true individual. Here we are a person of Being, a person of presence. Presence is manifesting itself as a person. But it is also a *human* person. A person, then, is not just spirit, but something additional to spirit. It is not just pure consciousness or awareness, but something more. The vastness or infinite expanse of impersonal emptiness or consciousness cannot be a person; only an individual being can be a person. However, these transcendent dimensions of true nature can express themselves as a person in the form of a human being, a person of the same quality as the fundamental consciousness. In the Hindu Vedas, this is recognized as the god Krishna, who is a person, not just an impersonal vastness like the Brahman. If pure consciousness or spirit does not manifest in individual beings it cannot know or experience itself, or express its qualities and wisdoms. A person is the acme of the development of a being.

The sense of presence in the personal essence is much more palpable than in any of the other aspects we discussed. It is unmistakable. Some people become concerned that they are gaining weight when they feel the hefty fullness in their belly and might reject this fullness of presence as reflecting excessive weight if there is no guidance. It is a palpable presence of pure consciousness that knows it is present and knows also it is a person. It is actually the answer to the question I asked before: Where did the soul learn about being an individual? It is from this prototype of personhood. It is also possible that children around the age of two experience this quality of presence as they begin separating from their parents and individuating, a normal process for all humans. If they do, they might not be aware of the presence. What will likely make a bigger impression is the sense of being a person. This sense can remain as an intuition or imprint around which the ego individual develops through the construction of images and structures. This might explain why all humans develop as individuals instead of as something else. Beyond being an individual, in Western civilizations particularly, people want to be their own person, unique and distinct. It is a sign of respect when one is treated as a person instead of as an entity or an object.

This presence of the personal essence is usually white and glistening, like a white pearl. So we also call it the pearl or the pearl beyond price. Not shiny or bright, it is luminescent, with a gentle glow that makes us feel we are being ourselves. The expression "I am" fits very well here, as does the expression "I am myself—authentic and real." The Sufis think of the center of the pearl as the center of the heart, what they call the *latifa ana'iya*, meaning it has to do with oneself, with self or identity. They refer to this center as the "most hidden" in order to point to the secret that lies there, a secret that is rarely known. We are our own person, autonomous and not dependent on anybody else. But the autonomy goes beyond a psychological stance, for we are a person independent of what the mind says, including our own mind. The process of making such a state accessible and established as a station is a long story, which is why I wrote a whole book about this aspect.[5]

CHARACTERISTICS OF THE PERSONAL ESSENCE

The ego ideal of type Three has little to do with being a real person. The ideal of the type is a shadow of what a real person can be. It is about being efficient, competent, and successful according to the model of a particular society or group. It takes some of the characteristics of the pearl and builds an image around them. However, the pearl, with all its characteristics, almost completely illuminates the shell of this type. To appreciate this, we need a fuller understanding of its core. Type Three wants to be successful, but successful as the exemplar of their group or society. The exemplar is an individual who has attained what the society has determined is meant by "having made it as a human being." This is a reflection of what the pearl stands for, for it is the exemplar of what a human being can be—not according to group standards, a tradition, a culture or its mores but according to a person's unique qualities of being, their true capacities and skills. It is uniqueness independent of any societal influence, even though there can be similarities to particular social mores for some human beings.

The true story of human success is finding the pearl, or maturing to the point of being able to embody it, rather than being successful in an external way or in the external world. Then we are truly human, a human who represents the divine, a vice-regent of the sacred, so to speak. We are also the window through which the divine looks into the world of manifestation while still remaining aware of its divinity. The pearl is a success story, for it is being a person like other human beings but also a person who expresses the spirit with all of its qualities. Both the Kabbalah and the Sufi teachings define their ideal not as the enlightenment of transcendence but as the complete or perfect human being. This person is seen as a bridge between the ordinary world and the divine world, a human who lives in the two worlds simultaneously. One is both nondual and dual, living life in both of these realms.

The pearl has the characteristic of personalness but also of contact. A true person can make contact simply by being oneself; they do not have to utter a word or do a thing. By one's presence alone contact takes place, and yet it does not exclude the other external ways of contacting others. The pearl is also the functional aspect of essence. It stands not just for personhood but for functional personhood. Part of this functionality is relational, and that is where the personal element and contact are important. But it also has to do with all kinds of functionality in the world. When we embody the pearl, then we are free from history while still being a person. We can function in the world in an effective and objective way, which makes the pearl efficient. Our functionality is efficient and attains excellence. This efficiency is not reserved for worldly functioning but also bridges the two worlds. We can function in the ordinary and divine worlds efficiently. Without the pearl we have no functionality in the invisible world of spirit beyond just being.

We can see that the Three type is attempting to imitate the true person of Being, but ends up instead with only an image of what that can be. They can be capable, but only in worldly things and in the area in which they succeed. The real person is capable wherever capacity is needed. The senses we explored with the other lataif—"I can" and "I will"—both belong to the pearl, to the truly matured and individuated soul, the "I am." The liberated Three embodies what is true in our spiritual nature, not just what is best in their culture or group. The liberated Three is the true model, not for a particular society but for all of humanity. Whoever embodies the pearl is the exemplar of humanity and the true model of what a human being can be. They are efficient, but about the right matters and in a way that recognizes other human beings as persons in their own right. They even recognize groups for what they are and relate to them with attunement to their uniqueness. The liberated Three can then contribute to society and to humanity as a whole. The prophet Mohammad was not a Three, but he was considered a complete man, the model of humanity. He was definitely a person; he acted as one and lived as one. He was connected directly to the divine, but he lived a human life. He was a reformer, a leader, a statesman, a husband, and a father. He came to his community to contribute to its deliverance from ignorance and barbarity into a true humane society. That is his legacy. But how many of his followers know that or attempt to see him as the exemplar? The Sufis and some of his other followers do. But for the rest, his message became a religion of laws and rules. For the real person there are no rules. Only inner reality dictates what is right and useful.

Some of the Hebrew prophets had this status, for it is the ideal of Hebrew spirituality. King Solomon is considered such. In our modern time, a good example of a developed but not enlightened Three is the former president of the United States, John F. Kennedy. He averted a nuclear war intelligently and served the country in many progressive ways. He embodied the nation's ideal but also many of humanity's ideals.

Instead of being a true person, implying a successful or completed spiritual path, the Three's attempts to emulate what it means to be a true human being turn the energy, dynamism, and efficiency of the inner practice to outward skills for outer goals. They certainly succeed in society. But the more fixated they are, the more they accomplish this success through deception of themselves and others. They become worshippers of the golden calf. And the capacity for being personal, relational, and contactual becomes simply a façade, a display, empty of the real fullness of the pearl. They might become famous—a movie or sports star—but they do not shine in their inner world. Their shine is worldly and fake.

Understanding the patterns of the fixation can help point us to the ego ideal. And by recognizing that this ideal is a facsimile constructed from the ideas and influences of the current time, we might be more open to the real aspect that is idealized. We might also understand how this aspect is attained through truth instead of lies and deception.

THE DIRECT APPROACH
TO PERSONAL ESSENCE

The direct approach is straightforward. We need to look at our capacity to be personal, at our capacity for contact and relating in a real way, and at our functionality. We also need to look at *how* we function. Do we function efficiently as a machine or as a human being with a heart? Do we attain with truth and integrity or with lies and half-truths? Do we consider others as persons in their own right or are they only a means for our success or mirrors for our excellence? We discern these questions by exploring what it is to be a person, a truly autonomous individual, not the self-made man or woman. A real person is a human being, free from the mind, the exigencies of time, and the influence of culture and family. It is not that one doesn't care for one's culture or family but that one relates to them as what we all truly are: as members of society, of course, but also genuine and authentic human beings before anything else. We are human before we are a man or woman, Black or white, nationalistic or ideological . . . or anything.

We look to see if we are this kind of person or can make this kind of personal contact. This inquiry may lead us to compassionately recognize the fact that we are not, that we are a fake or an imitation. As we see our fakeness and our falsehood, we arrive at the disconnection from being a true person. We discover the emptiness underlying the fake, empty shell. The Enneagram of avoidances describes the avoidance of type Three as failure or hopelessness. This is reminiscent of the specific difficulty that is part of the core of this fixation. Valuing this emptiness and welcoming it as the truth helps us free ourselves from the way we pretend. We become open to the arising of the true person that we are. We are perhaps ready and mature enough to become the pearl beyond price.

To experience the personal essence is one thing; to have permanent access to it is another. This access requires maturation, which means discerning and integrating the truth from all aspects of our life, the metabolism of the meaning in our experiences. It requires us to examine our life so that it is completely transparent and its truth clear and definite. This truth is what feeds the soul as it grows and matures. This maturation becomes an essential individuation, culminating in the station of the pearl beyond price, the royalty of the inner realm.

7

Point Four
ESSENTIAL IDENTITY

Type Four is the tragic type known for their melancholy and grief. They tend to be sad and dramatic, as if always missing something essential in themselves. Fours behave as if they have been separated from a beloved they can no longer find, so they pine away, though sometimes not knowing for what. They feel convinced of their originality, specialness, and aesthetic acumen. Their model is the archetypal suffering artist, talented but overlooked, abandoned and unable to find their way to a contented life. Vincent van Gogh is probably a good example of this type. As are Joni Mitchell and Katharine Hepburn. The Four is known as the Individualist (Ego-Melan in Ichazo's original language). Hudson and Riso write the following:

> Fours often report that they feel they are missing something in themselves, although they may have difficulty identifying exactly what that something is. Is it willpower? Social ease? Self-confidence? Emotional tranquility?—all of which they see in others, seemingly in abundance. Given time and sufficient perspective, Fours generally recognize that they are unsure about aspects of their self-image—their

personality or ego structure itself. They feel that they lack a clear and stable identity, particularly a social persona that they feel comfortable with.[1]

This lack of a stable identity contributes to the need to be special, sometimes "most special." Yet if they do have some stable sense of self, they can also be strong and determined, dauntless and unafraid of challenges. This is why the Enneagram of idealizations describes their ego ideal as "I am diligent" and "I am the elite and know what's what." The Four's tendency, though, is to try to control themselves and their circumstances. This creates a conflict because control runs counter to their idealization of spontaneity and originality. They need control, for control is a way to support an unstable sense of who they are, yet they yearn for the originality they feel is their birthright. Originality, authenticity, specialness, and related characteristics form their ego ideal and are a reflection or expression of their idealized aspect. They actually idealize their special endowment, the particular aspect that is their birthright, but they don't know what it truly is. Rather, they have some obscure feeling or intuition of it around which they construct their ideal of originality. This is true for all types. They idealize their particular essential endowment without actually knowing what it is. Instead they feel some vague reflection of it and from this they build an ideal that patterns the shell of their fixation.

Sandra Maitri writes of this type,

> Fours want to be seen as unique, original, aesthetic, and creative; and being one of the image types—present themselves in this way. They value their refined taste and sensitivity, which they usually feel is deeper and more profound than that of others.[2]

Their envy of others can express itself as harsh self-judgment, even self-hatred, but they still maintain a self-image of being special—almost chosen—in some secret way. That is why we find some Fours believing they are the second coming, or the messiah. A famous example is the Jewish rabbi, Sabbatai Zevi, who believed he was the awaited Jewish messiah. His sense of grandiose raja specialness got him imprisoned by the Ottoman sultan, who he went to in order to convert him to Judaism.

THE IDEALIZED ASPECT:
ESSENTIAL IDENTITY

Fixated Fours experience themselves as more than an individual with some differentiating characteristics. At the center of their sense of individuality, their sense of self, is a feeling of identity, of who they are. This is true of ego in general, for ego is the soul that became structured as an individual with a sense of identity. You can be an individual and not have a sense of who you are, but the feeling of identity provides the emotional and conceptual marker that tells you who you are through the changes of life and the passage of years. It is always you, regardless of the changes that occur during encounters with life situations.

Modern depth psychology has shown that issues around our sense of identity can be destabilizing and make us more sensitive and narcissistic.[3] The extent of instability around our sense of self determines our degree of narcissism, which the Diamond Approach understands as the distance our identity is from who we really are.[4]

In spiritual teachings in general, we don't find a clear distinction between the individuality of ego and its identity. They are conflated as the ego or the self that stands in the way of our realization. We see this in the following, where Naranjo correctly describes the particular estrangement of type Four as follows: "Yet, more basically, the pursuit of being through the emulation of the self-ideal stands on a basis of self-rejection and of blindness to the value of one's true self."[5]

While this is true, it lacks the specificity we need for our work, especially if we are to understand the idealized aspect of this type. Most teachings do not even conceptualize identity, except perhaps as the ultimate self, that one's true identity is Brahman or Shiva, or "I am that." It is difficult to find a teaching that acknowledges a true essential identity of the soul or individual consciousness that is unique to it and, hence, different from other souls' identities. There are exceptions in some Sufi teachings that characterize the true self as a star, or in some of the raja yogas that recognize the *atman* as a shining star. The nondual sense of "infinite self" as one's identity does not particularly help in understanding the Four type because this is true for all types. Nisargadatta Maharaj, a teacher of nondualistic Vedanta, does discuss the point of light, but he says nothing about its relation to identity or self.

PRESENCE OF ESSENTIAL IDENTITY

There is an essential presence that is experienced as a point of light, a presence that many teachings know, but most of them are oblivious to its importance as the identity of the soul. For them, it is related to the infinite self of nonduality, like Brahman, Shiva, or the *keter* of Kabbalah. In the Diamond Approach, we see it as an essential aspect that reveals the true identity of the soul and for point Four it is the source of their idealization. It is possible that they felt its presence as children but did not know what they were experiencing, even though they might have felt the sense of identity and its associated characteristics of specialness, originality, and authenticity. It is their true endowment, so they probably had more sense of it as children than other types.

Many teachings report the experience of a point of light that shines like a star, usually emerging at first glimpse like a shooting star. But then it might appear zipping around our consciousness without us knowing what it is, even though we can be taken by its radiance and sparkle. It is mostly recognized or experienced by those who have some inner vision, since the feeling by itself does not evoke the sense of a shining star, but rather, of a point of presence. However, if our feeling sense of it is sustained, we may recognize what it feels like and what it stands for.

It is true that it feels like presence concentrated in a point, the way Nisargadatta Maharaj knew and described it. But we may then recognize that it has in it another affect besides the self-knowing as a point of presence. This affect is an essential sense of "I," a definite feeling of identity. It is a feeling or affect of identity that is not learned or borrowed but inherent to it. Hence it naturally has the knowledge of itself as self, as "I," as identity that is irreducible and impossible to explain by other things. The point of presence is not a construct or mental knowledge; it is gnostic, immediate knowing of the point, of what it is. This also shows that the sense of identity, the sense of "I," is a Platonic idea, not created by mind or borrowed from others.

This is not unlike the knowing of all other essential aspects, where the knowing is inherent to it and inseparable from the knowing of presence. It is a presence with a particular affect, here one of identity. We need intimacy or closeness in the experience of our essential point to recognize the unfabricated affect of identity, the pure feeling of I-ness. As we study it further, we see how it has the sense of authenticity, for it is authentically what we are—our true nature as our identity. The most complete experience of the point of light and presence is not a matter of seeing or feeling it but of being it. This transition from experiencing to being is a quantum leap in our spiritual development, for spirit here is what we are, not what we have or what we experience. It is the movement from spiritual experience to spiritual realization, realizing we are the point and experiencing ourselves as such.

The realization is amazing. We feel we are a center of light and wisdom, a singularity of presence that radiates all qualities and aspects as part of its radiance. Yet each person or soul has a different radiance, not only in the intensity of it or how big or concentrated the point is but in what rays of light it emanates. Some have a slight blue tinge to them, others a hint of pink or golden love. Some emit a green radiance, making them more compassionate and kind. There are an infinite number of combinations, making each person's point unique, although every point is primarily white brilliance. The point turns out to give us the sense of uniqueness that the type Four idealizes and believes makes them special.

When we experience ourselves as the point or the essential identity, we feel we are authentically ourselves, with the certainty of direct divine knowledge. As the point, we can feel like a dense, full concentration or a bright point of light. We can feel the point so completely that we no longer discern it as a point because we are subsumed within it. Sometimes we can even lose the sense of "I." This realization gives us a new capacity, making it possible for us to experience any essential presence or quality as what we are. We no longer experience spirit; we *are* spirit, regardless of what quality it takes. In the Diamond Approach, we recognize the importance of the point in our spiritual process, so it is remarkable to us that many teachers and teachings do not see it.

They experience some manifestation of presence as who they are and usually stop at that.

The qualities we experience in being the point are freedom, spaciousness, lightness, playfulness, uniqueness, and authenticity. We are definitely what we are. The "who" and "what" of the soul become one. As the point, we can feel stationary, or we can zoom around our personal consciousness or even the vastness of universal cosmic consciousness. The point can arise in any part of the body or anywhere in our individual consciousness, and we recognize it as the unique, essential identity of our soul. It can fill our soul with radiant, joyful light, while also centering it and giving it the feeling of stability and integrity.

CHARACTERISTICS OF ESSENTIAL IDENTITY

Fours have lost contact with their essential identity, so they seek it through the idealization of some of its characteristics. Exploring the essential identity and relating it to the patterns of this type, we can see how the idealization has patterned the shell of this fixation. Since the point is the center of the soul, it feels like our origin and nucleus. Because the point is, in some deep way, the origin of the soul and its qualities and faculties, Fours are interested in originality. The point also shines the ground of Being into the soul—the universal origin of all—and so its realization readily beckons us to move deeper into this fundamental origin. But for fixated Fours, originality has lost its true source, and so it is self-centered and possessed by the ego. For the point, originality is simply the origin of one's qualities and the center of one's being with no possession or self-centeredness. The more liberated the Four, the more the question of originality becomes a yearning for the origin rather than for being unique, and this brings the understanding that being original is not self-centered. This yearning for originality is a significant Four pattern that can create the melancholy and grief, as well as the depression, that characterize many of this type.

Since the point is the individual essential expression of the world of spirit in its entirety, one's separation from it feels like an enormous loss, even though Fours may not quite know what they have lost. It can feel like the loss of home or something precious, and the longing for it elicits a deep sadness. The longing is actually for the inner beloved, which is our true being in its universal and cosmic infinity. The point of light can be seen as the expression of this transcendent truth in the individual soul. But Fours do not usually know this and believe the longing is for any number of other things. The more aware Fours become, the more they realize that what is missing is inward.

The yearning for authenticity is actually a direct longing and movement toward the point of being. As the point we feel we are not just authentically ourselves but authenticity itself. But the feeling of authenticity that Fours idealize becomes the distorted belief and self-centered conviction that they are original and creative or that their creativity is special, authentic, and better than that of others. A trace of this in Fours and all other types is the feeling that what one creates, artistically or otherwise, is special and authentic. But most often this feeling is because they made it themselves and not because the creation has value in itself.

The creativity is partly an imitation of the point's radiance of many qualities and colors, expressing the universal creativity of the transcendent and universal spirit, which is constantly unfolding the universe.[6] Fours feel special because the point is what is truly special about us. It is the specialness, the preciousness of our spiritual nature, and the point is the aspect that reveals this truth most explicitly. The longing or aspiration for specialness is the longing for the point of light combined with a sense or feeling of its absence in our experience. This longing in the Four is a major pattern that reflects the idealization of the point and gives us some indication of what it is that is obscured by ideas and history.

The drama, on the other hand, is the opposite of what the point is and what it feels like. The idealization of authenticity and originality becomes dramatic. It appears in intimate and social relationships as dramatic expressions and actions. Good examples from Hollywood are two actors who appeared in major dramatic movies: Peter O'Toole, who played Lawrence of Arabia, and Richard Burton, whose marriage to Elizabeth Taylor had all the drama of the Four's tragedy. Elizabeth Taylor herself was probably a Four. This drama, as a part of one's originality, moves further away from the idealized aspect and more toward the distorted reflections of the point. The point has the sense of simplicity and ordinariness that is the essence of being authentically who we are. When we are authentically who we are, we have no need to be seen or to express who we are in dramatic ways that draw attention. We are content in simply being, with no fanfare or drama, no need or desire for dramatic colors or expressions. We would rather be seen as an ordinary person who does not stand out. But Fours want to stand out, to have their specialness reflected, and they try to ensure this through their creativity in drama, dance, art, and poetry. They can be good artists, and the closer they are to the idealized quality the more their creativity—be it their poetry, music, painting, or acting—expresses something more meaningful and profound.

By identifying these major patterns of the type, especially understanding them as expressions of an idealization, we can approach the possibility of finding the idealized quality of presence. More exactly, by actually recognizing our idealization and understanding it as an imitation or a reflection of something real and more profound, we open to the emergence of the actual idealized aspect of the point of light. This can have two important results for Fours: First, there is more liberation from the limiting and confining patterns of the fixation—more joy and freedom and true authenticity. Secondly, and even more important, Fours may discover the essential quality that they are idealizing. Recognizing this means seeing their true spiritual spark and realizing that if they are truly themselves, they have the possibility to reside in the origin of things. This is spiritual awakening, not merely liberation from the psychological patterns of the type. The awakened Four is a light for others, a true expression of how Being gives focus and meaning to a human life. Their feelings come from their essential heart and their actions from the center of their true being.

THE DIRECT APPROACH TO ESSENTIAL IDENTITY

Discovering their essential quality can be harder for Fours than for many of the other types. The point of light and presence—the essential identity—is a quality of essence that is more central, similar in its centrality to the pearl beyond price. But the barriers against it are more difficult and need more courage and maturity to penetrate. Even so, the path is the same as that of the other aspects. We need to recognize first what our familiar identity or sense of identity is like—what it feels like and what it is built upon. We need to explore it until we see its constructed mental nature. This is not easy because we believe it is really what we are and resist seeing that it might not be. To grasp our identity as a mental construct is quite threatening. It brings up our narcissism, which we all have as long as we identify with the image defined by our ego fixation.

Confronting our sense of identity threatens us and makes us feel more vulnerable and shaky. This shakiness brings up our narcissistic tendencies, such as the need to be seen and, more specifically, to be seen as special or important. It rekindles the hurt and anger we felt for not getting this acknowledgment in our early history. It also brings up all the ways we try to shore up our sense of identity, all the strategies we employ to support our identity so that it does not reveal its flimsy nature. It can force us to realize how our idealization of others helps us feel supported just by being associated with them and also how we need to be idealized and admired. These are very emotionally sensitive areas, and many people cannot really grapple with them without expert help, by which I mean that of a skilled therapist or an attuned and psychologically informed spiritual guide.

If we can recognize our usual sense of identity and see its constructed mental nature, it will bring up, as usual, our disconnection from our essential identity. We usually do not know what we are disconnected from; we simply feel not real, fake, false. If we can sense into the disconnection more completely, we will feel lost, not knowing who or what we are, or disoriented, not knowing how to act in our lives. That is why the Enneagram of avoidances identifies despair and feeling lost as the things that Fours most try to avoid. If we have skilled support or are able to tolerate such states and stay with them as part of our ongoing inquiry and practice, we might begin to feel the emptiness that signifies the absence or lack of essential identity. It is a feeling of being empty and without substance, coupled with a sense of not knowing what our real identity is.

By being patient and compassionate with ourselves in remaining with this kind of emptiness, it can transform into a peaceful spaciousness where there is no sense of self, yet also no suffering about it. Remaining in this silent peacefulness, the point of light can then arise or descend in our consciousness. This allows us to either recognize it as our true sense of identity or become it, to feel ourselves as being true and authentic. We feel we are being who and what we truly are. There are many permutations of our sense of the point. We can experience ourselves explicitly as a point of light and presence. We might feel the sense of preciousness that does not require external mirroring and reflection, or even the sense of timelessness of our true being. We are then certain of who we are and free to be ourselves—not the product of our history, but spontaneously and naturally what we are in the very moment.

Notice here that it is not only knowing or experiencing presence or simply being in the now. It is a more particular and specific sense of presence and nowness. It is both an identity and a timeless sense of being or presence.[7] At the same time, as we realize and integrate this essential identity, we become free from the patterns of the Four type, and we realize the qualities and characteristics behind the idealization. We are authentic, special in an ordinary way that does not require the limelight or applause, deep and profound without having to announce it to others or create dramas around it. We are original by simply being ourselves, and our creativity tends to be naturally and spontaneously original, without us having to seek out originality. We are complete, and our expressions are true and authentic. We live simply in freedom that does not seek recognition. This is true inner freedom.

8

Point Seven
PLEASURE VEHICLE

Point Sevens are the dilettantes. They sample many things they believe will bring them happiness and pleasure. But they are after stimulation and immediate gratification, and the more fixated Sevens rarely settle on one thing long enough to truly savor it. Sevens are always planning the future they believe will give them the happiness and pleasure that will satisfy them. Hence Ichazo's original name for this type: Ego-Plan. But, as usual, this is their specific reaction, which focuses on the ego ideal as the way to regain the condition of unconditional love and holding that they've lost touch with.

Sandra Maitri describes the main traits of the Seven type as follows:

> Sevens are buoyant, perky, optimistic, curious, interested in everything, youthful in spirit, futuristic, and seem always to be one step ahead of themselves. Seemingly more carefree than the other types, Sevens use these very qualities as their biggest defense. They need the stimulation of new ideas, experiences, entertainment and other pursuits, and get easily bored and dissatisfied when things become repetitive.[1]

Russ Hudson and Don Riso elaborate in a more positive tone characteristics of the more developed Sevens:

> We have named this personality type the *Enthusiast* because Sevens are enthusiastic about almost everything that catches their attention. They approach life with curiosity, optimism, and a sense of adventure, like kids in a candy store who look at the world in wide-eyed, rapt anticipation of all the good things they are about to experience. They are bold and vivacious, pursuing what they want in life with cheerful determination.[2]

Both of these descriptions accurately reflect this type's traits and behavior patterns and also reveal the ego ideal clearly, which, when we look more closely, points to the idealized quality with which Sevens have lost connection. Many of these traits are either reflections of this spiritual quality or approximations of it. Some of them are a direct expression of it but in a distorted or ignorant way that actually leads Sevens away from the dynamics of their core. Which is why they are perpetually seeking that elusive satisfaction that never seems to last, even when they think they have found it. The Enneagram of idealizations describes the ego ideal as "I am okay" and "I am not suffering."

The ego ideal of the Seven is one of optimism and positivity, based on this self-image of "okayness." But it is more than just okayness; it is pleasure and adventure, lightness and delight. Sevens idealize the ability to discover, create, and imagine magical, fascinating worlds and endless opportunities for enjoyment and pleasure. They shun suffering and pain as merely the wrong perspective on life or one's situation. Instead they prefer to look forward to what delights life will bring, and should life disappoint, they simply shift course and aim for some new possibility. They see their strength as one of not being pinned down or limited, always keeping the door open to move on if things get too dark. And yet they can manifest a drive for consuming new experiences that belies their easygoing self-image.

THE IDEALIZED ASPECT:
PLEASURE VEHICLE

It is amazing how close Sevens are to the spiritual quality they idealize and yet how far they can be from actually experiencing and knowing it as it is. It is not an easy quality to access, since it is not simply a quality of spirit, or what we call an essential aspect. It is a grouping of the essential qualities together in a particular configuration that we term a "diamond vehicle."

Diamond vehicles are carriers of wisdom about various elements in the nature of the soul and its journey of unfoldment. This particular vehicle requires what the Sufis refer to as the latifa of *qalb*, or heart, which they associate with the prophet Abraham and the color yellow. The center of this quality of joy is a place slightly above the left nipple (just as the red of strength is at the right side and the white at the solar plexus). It might open for some people, without them noticing, when they are happy in a carefree way, especially when they are not concerned about anything and are relaxed and at ease. Usually, however, the moment we notice we are joyful, it tends to close down, for the quality of joy is extremely subtle and vulnerable to the mind and emotional reactions. It is actually, in this respect, the most subtle of the lataif.

When the center first opens, we can see a yellow transparent sun in the middle. It is not intense like our usual sun, but delicate, subtle, and beautiful—a radiant sun with a gentle yellow luminosity. The affect is unadulterated joy, an expansive lightness and delight that seems to be about nothing. It reminds us of feeling happy, but it is so ethereal that it does not correspond to the mind's usual conditions for being happy. Reactions of the personality tend to close it down, which is one reason it is difficult for people to be happy. Yet joy is not the exact quality for this type; it is actually just one ingredient of it, even though it gives a rough feeling of what it is. This is a discrimination that requires a great deal of spiritual experience and discernment to recognize. However, if Sevens access and integrate their essential endowment, the diamond vehicle of pleasure—which includes joy—the key to unlocking the secrets of the fixation is available and can take them deeper, helping them to unravel the inner core.

PRESENCE OF THE MARKABAH

It is ordinarily difficult to experience and recognize the presence of this quality of our being, this diamond vehicle of pleasure, which we call the Markabah, for it is deep and expresses itself through many forms. The Markabah actually comprises all of the essential qualities arranged in a particular configuration, each expressing a particular flavor of pleasure or bliss. When we first feel it, we experience a presence of fullness or density—a rich, satisfying sense of being that is different from love or joy or fulfillment, though all are implicit in this presence. When savored and discerned directly, the quality that is in the foreground can only be called pleasure—a sweet, tangy, yummy pleasure that is at the same time sacred and profound such that it can easily be referred to as bliss or ecstasy.

This vehicle has two modes, with one of them dominating our experience at any given time. The deeper mode feels like profound inner pleasure of many kinds, where the presence has the sense of fullness and richness. The other mode is experienced more as externally expressive, and it feels expansive and celebratory, like a happy celebration filled with song and dance. It is playful and light.

Unlike the qualities we have discussed so far, we can feel the Markabah as either the full presence of the vehicle or as the presence of one specific aspect of the vehicle manifesting as pleasure. Each aspect here manifests as its own quality but also as the pleasure of experiencing this quality. It is easier to feel one aspect at a time, for the vehicle is profound and its realization requires deep work and spiritual openness. The significant fact is that this form of presence can appear as many kinds of pleasure or ecstatic bliss. Sweetness is always part of the pleasure of the presence, as if each presence is permeated by a heavenly sweetness that adds to its pleasure. This combination of sweetness and bliss clearly centers this presence in the heart. But each quality has its particular flavor of sweetness. The yellow joy tastes like sugar, the black peace like licorice, the fulfillment quality like apricot, the green kindness like mint, and so on. We can taste the sweetness on our tongue or in our mouth. But we can also taste it at the sight of the presence, whether it appears in the chest, the head, or other parts of the body. The inner capacity of taste is not localized orally like our physical tasting. We can taste a quality anywhere it is present.

This is always the case for any quality of presence, for it is part of the secret, or mystery, of presence. The presence of the quality, the knowing of the quality, the sensation of the quality, the texture of the quality, the taste of the quality, and even the sound of the quality are all at the site of the presence of the quality. Because presence itself is an expression of pure consciousness before it differentiates into the sense modalities, in its knowingness it always possesses a property called synesthesia that includes all the sense modalities. Synesthesia is a physical condition in which stimulation of one sensory modality may be perceived through a different modality—for instance, sound is tasted or a color is heard. Here we refer to the fact that in presence, experience is not yet differentiated into different sensory modalities so the different modalities may not appear as separate. Each and all qualities of essential presence inherently have this synesthetic property, but not every soul has developed the capacity for spiritual synesthesia. Some sense, some see, some taste, and some have more than one capacity for knowing. Of course, the knowing of the quality is inherent in the quality as both cognition and affect, but it includes all the ways in which this aspect of consciousness can express itself through the various senses.

Besides tasting and seeing it, we can also sense it, and in this sensing we feel the texture of presence. We can sense and see either each particular quality of pleasure individually or the vehicle as a whole with its majestic beauty and glamorous colors. We will see as we explore the patterns of this type how the different qualities of pleasure can be used to illuminate these patterns and traits of the Seven.

The Markabah can feel light and bubbly, playful with various shifting qualities of delight. Or it can manifest as a deep and rich pleasure, profoundly satisfying. It is actually the *essence* of pleasure, delight, and happiness. Most people are not familiar with deep pleasure like this and certainly not as part of our spiritual nature or the expression of its richness. The Markabah, which comes from the Hebrew word for chariot or carousel, can appear wherever you are as filling the whole space, accompanied by heavenly music and the sight of twirling diamonds of different colors. Or it can manifest within our individual subjectivity as either lightness or deep richness. The lightness tends to be celebrative and joyful, and the depth as pleasurable and satisfying. Usually, it is not easy to discern these manifestations of our spiritual nature if we are only familiar with the infinite ground of nondual experiencing. But it is possible if we are open and working on the issues that block or distort pleasure, whether we are in a nondual condition or the ordinary individual condition.

This vehicle is connected with the heart, so it tends to occupy the whole chest, but it can fill the whole body or expand beyond it. Like all other qualities of our spiritual nature, there is no actual size associated with it. This vehicle shows us that pleasure, delight, and bliss come in a variety of forms, each expressing something profound about our nature, and it shows how each form is needed for our life and inner path.

CHARACTERISTICS
OF THE MARKABAH

We can see the patterns of the shell of the fixation from the characteristics associated with the quality of pleasure but also understand some of them from the presence of the quality itself. We will also see how many of the Seven's traits attempt to experience and express pleasure or happiness but in a distorted, incomplete, or inauthentic manner. The seeking of pleasure and enjoyment is a direct seeking of the quality, but the seeking is external. The belief is that it comes from the objects and situations of life. But true, unadulterated pleasure is a quality of our own being. We just need to be ourselves freely, in a carefree way. If we turn inward deeply, ecstatic pleasure will naturally be there. This bliss is experienced as the affect of authenticity, the actual feel of reality. Even when it comes as a response to enjoying something external, we are actually feeling inner joy or pleasure because the attainment of that external thing has quieted our mind and settled our heart enough for the inner delight to manifest. But that inner delight is short-lived when it is not recognized for what it is—if it is known as an emotional feeling resulting from external circumstances rather than the direct experience of our being. Sevens tend to think such delight comes from external sources or activities, not trusting that it is part of being who they truly are. But most people, no matter their type, believe this about pleasure. It is Sevens who exemplify it most clearly.

The fact is that Sevens are head-centered, and so pleasure tends to be connected to content, ideas, situations, and people, and they find it hard to rest in the contentless nature of essential pleasure. They cannot trust their own heart and belly because these lead them into the underlying emptiness and the loss of the pleasure and stimulation they believe they need to survive. This reliance on their mind and its ability to direct their experience tends to distance them from the basic goodness and bliss inherent in simply being what they are.

The mental orientation of Sevens can become real, and then it is a matter of discovering many things about reality. An example of such is the prodigious discoverer and author Sri Aurobindo. It is clear from his writings that he was mentally oriented, but the mind was used in the service of discovering the truths about reality and consciousness. He was a modern pioneer of the adventure of consciousness.

The sense of buoyancy, joie de vivre, enthusiasm, and bubbliness of the Seven ideal can be a true expression of this inner pleasure, but these qualities usually arise as responses to enjoying something in life—a person, a dish, a movie, an idea, an activity, and so on. This can happen with essential pleasure or joy, but for the awakened individual, it is clear that the feeling originates from within; it is not caused by external stimuli. It does not need any situation or activity for it to manifest because it is the luster of our authenticity. And the quality of pleasure and delight usually responds to a life situation or particulars of the inner process.

The characteristics associated with the vehicle of pleasure can help us understand more of the traits of the Seven. One of these is playfulness and mirth. It is natural to be playful when free, not in the sense of playing a game but in feeling lighthearted, in interacting spontaneously in activities, and in the playful attitude we have about life in general. The fact that this vehicle encompasses many kinds of pleasure and delight can explain why Sevens tend to jump around from one thing to another in search of pleasurable tastes in various situations and activities. There are always more things to try that could be more pleasurable than the last. True seeking of bliss requires us to turn inward to the true source of pleasure. If we do that, we find that whatever pleasure or delight we experience in life is simply a reflection of its essential counterpart, which is found to be more profound, pure, and causeless. Sevens, however, are curious mostly about the surface of things, what they can touch and see and taste, not about themselves or the inner meaning of reality. They are drawn to what they think will make them feel good, as if happiness is the only worthwhile quality in a full life. Even in work they try many things, becoming interested in a skill or project but often moving on to something else before they master it. The satisfaction they derive from work, a person, an activity, or a creative pursuit is always short-lived. This kind of curiosity, of course, does not lead to depth and satisfaction, so they remain dilettantes, stuck at the surface level of things.

An important distinction is that authentic seeking is about inquiring in order to find the truth. For Sevens, it is about stimulation, about distracting themselves from reality by feeling good, high, or just hanging out. And since true curiosity or practice investigates with honesty and faithfulness—without the agenda of a goal or a specific state of any kind—experience is bound to change and unfold on its own. So, inquiry moves on to the new arising organically—the way truth unfolds experience to reveal its deeper truth. In contrast, Sevens move on to another area or thing because the first loses its luster, its interest, and it no longer satisfies, not because it is what is naturally arising in their exploration. What activates our curiosity is whatever reveals the truth—for example, the truth of encounters we do not understand, yet know to be important to comprehend because of their significance in our lives and to our inner development. True curiosity, which fuels the inner search, seems to have its own eyes, its own truth sense. It directs us naturally to whatever the next thing is that we must experience and fathom. It does not move by chance or by our desires or by the pressure to avoid our emptiness or pain.

Sevens, however, definitely do. They want to experience what feels pleasurable, what tastes heavenly, while avoiding or denying whenever possible whatever is painful, difficult, or heavy. Again, this reflects what they are lacking: the quality of inner pleasure in its various manifestations. The fact is that if we follow true curiosity and inquiry it will lead to our true nature, which feels good and is truly heavenly because it is an expression of the spiritual world. That journey goes through difficulties and challenges, and it requires focus, patience, and commitment to follow the course until the truth is revealed, whether it is painful or wonderful. It also requires loyalty to the inner search and the essential, spiritual truth.

The incessant, endless desire for stimulating experiences and situations reflects an inner absence of the pleasure that is inherent to our consciousness and being. But Sevens do not want to look at, or even acknowledge, this absence; their allegiance is to worldly delights. Sevens can express this dilettantism even in their spiritual search, sampling teachings forever, instead of settling at some point on one that they go into deeply, with commitment and inner loyalty. They idealize their omnivorous impulse as an openness to variety and possibility, an optimism about unlimited opportunities for joy and delight. We can see how the varieties of delight and pleasure inherent in the Markabah are reflected here, but in external or superficial orientation.

This idealization camouflages the inner, seemingly endless emptiness that does not know what is really missing, or what will truly provide fulfillment and lasting, satisfying pleasure. For Sevens, the inner treasure of delights is hidden by this emptiness, so they see no source of pleasure inside. Yet only by turning inward and confronting this emptiness can Sevens find the true bliss of freedom.

The inner path of the Great Work is the supreme adventure that naturally moves through challenges and victories, frustrations and fulfillment, to finally reach an unfettered freedom whose joy and delight have no end. Sevens may derive a sense of adventure from their promiscuous experimentation, but it is a facsimile of this true adventure—the adventure of consciousness discovering what it is, what its secrets are, what the meaning of life is, and the possibilities inherent in living a human life.

By sincerely inquiring and investigating the Seven's character traits and behavior patterns, we can come to understand in our bones and flesh how these traits deviate from the straight arrow of truth. We can see how they are facsimiles of a kind of pleasure we do not know but may intuit or obscurely sense. The greater the sincerity, the more chance there is that we will see the ego ideal as an idea in the mind, a picture of what Sevens want to be and live. Their character traits point to a particular ego ideal. By seeing the ideal as a false concept—one based on obscure feelings and patterned by early experiences, difficulties and promises from the culture, or other sources—we become open to recognizing what Sevens are trying to imitate, to be, and to live. If we recognize that, then we have access to the key that will unlock this obstinate fixation and aid us in penetrating its core.

THE DIRECT APPROACH
TO THE MARKABAH

If experientially recognizing our ego ideal and the ways it patterns our character does not point us to our true essential quality, then we can directly approach the vehicle or the spiritual form itself and its characteristics. It is a matter of finding the sense of disconnection from the true quality in our experience. This is always the direct path for all qualities, even if a quality arises before we experience its lack, which happens sometimes on the path because presence tends to reveal its treasures when we attend to it with commitment and reverence. For instance, we might feel true bliss sometimes, but if we do not deal with our disconnection from it we cannot integrate it. Instead, we will only have occasional flashes of the quality (what Sufis call states), rather than open access to it (the more stable stations). By integrating an aspect into our being and identity, it becomes a station and not an occasional state. The Sufis consider the occasional experience a gift from the unseen world, but the station as the fruition we earn from our practice and work. This is true about all qualities and not just this particular form of true nature.

The work is a matter of looking at the traits: the dilettantism, the hunger for experiences, the need to jump around from one thing to another, the attitude of consumption, and the desire for always feeling good. Naranjo elucidates the latter characteristic of this type as follows:

Ontic deficiency is not only the source of hedonism (and pain avoidance) ... but also its consequence; for the confusion between love and pleasure fails to bring about the deeper meaningfulness than that of the immediately available. A sense of inner scarcity is also, of course, supported by alienation of the individual from his experiential depth, which occurs as a consequence of the hedonistic need to experience only what is pleasing.[3]

We need to feel what is behind these traits and/or what is happening in our consciousness when we engage in such behaviors, thoughts, or desires. Looking at the feelings and the inner states that the Seven's traits and behaviors defend against, we may come upon the underlying emptiness, the hungry barrenness devoid of pleasure, sweetness, and light. The Enneagram of avoidances identifies "pain" as the main avoidance of the Seven. The only way to deeper truth is to confront this emptiness that makes us feel depressed and heavy, unhappy and sad. Becoming friends with our sadness and our wounds helps lead us to this emptiness, which is the doorway to the true delight of being. We can use our curiosity in an earnest way to delve deeply into our need and our avoidance of pain in order to find out what these deep feelings are about.

At some point, we reach the place of experiencing this emptiness as the absence of pleasure. It is helpful for us to recognize that this is a transitional state and not the final end. Otherwise we will tend to be too scared to approach the absence with an open mind and heart. Welcoming this state as a desired guest can help ease our fear and provide a more helpful antidote than trying to cover the absence over with activities that make us feel good, distracting ourselves by planning for better futures, or avoiding or denying the suffering inside. We remain with it and question what its content and origins are. The history behind it can emerge, at which point we will need a lot of sincerity in our curiosity to inquire into what arises. This can be difficult for Sevens as they have built so much of their identity on denying their suffering.

Remaining in this emptiness, lacking pleasure, love, or happiness and not fighting or avoiding it in any way allows the deficient emptiness to transform on its own into a clear emptiness, spacious and pleasant. While it can feel good, we still need to stay there and not assume this is the end of our inquiry. As we sit with this state, the actual quality of pleasure has a chance to emerge and pervade the spaciousness, helping us feel the quality or presence of an unadulterated delight and deep satisfaction. This is the satisfaction of the heart and the happiness of the soul, delighting in being ourselves or simply enjoying reality and life. This can carry over to enjoying the particulars of our life but now as an expression of our true being instead of a defense against a hungry emptiness. We find that each situation evokes a different quality of pleasure, with its own color, sweetness, and texture.

Even when we have arrived at this place, we can keep exploring here and there whenever the manifestations of the fixation arise, until this quality of pleasure in its variety becomes a station, accessible to us naturally and consistently. Now we have the key to the type, which gives us a great deal of power and skill in tackling the shell and penetrating the core. If we have explored types Six and Eight, we might also have will and strength, respectively, providing us with two more of the nine keys and giving our inquiry and study a greater efficacy and power.

Another direct route to this vehicle in its entirety is looking at our allegiance, our loyalty. Are we seeking pleasure or the inner truth? The more we are loyal to the inner truth, regardless of what it is, the closer we are to the Markabah. It is the turn inward, the loyalty to the path of inner truth, that can become the shortest route to this multifaceted vehicle of delight and pleasure. Awakened Sevens, such as Sri Aurobindo, manifest this vehicle in their love of understanding and knowing the different ways our essential nature manifests. For it is the turning inward toward the truth that reveals itself as the soul's greatest pleasure—coming home to itself. This discovery can be so deep it can lead to realization and some degree of liberation. This is true for all types, but the Markabah, the vehicle of essential pleasure, is particular to the Seven type, and so it is most important for them to examine where their true loyalties and priorities lie.

9

Point Nine
BOUNDLESS LOVE

Type Nine is the source of all other types and embodies the primary element inherent in all fixations. This is the element of sleep. What does sleep mean here? It means that Nines are asleep to what reality actually is, as well as being unconscious of who they truly are. They are asleep to the essential in life and give more attention to the external, peripheral, and superficial than to their interior depth. This is true of all fixated types and, hence, this Nine trait pervades all the fixations.

Fixated Nines can be understood as being numb to what they feel, to what is important and significant, which is why they are constantly seeking distraction and busy hoarding and collecting. Ichazo calls the type Ego-Indolence, and it is also known as the Peacemaker. To understand the Nine's ego ideal, we need to look at their other traits and dynamics. Maitri describes them as follows:

> Rarely asserting themselves, they like keeping things harmonious and pleasant, and have difficulty doing or saying anything that others might find offensive, uncomfortable, or controversial. So, they shun confrontations,

rarely express negative feelings or opinions, and focus on the positive. They are excellent mediators, able to see everyone's point of view, but often have difficulty discerning and expressing their own.[1]

Naranjo elaborates further:

> The combination of loss of interiority and the resigned and abnegated character that goes along with it results in a syndrome of a good-hearted, comfortable "earthiness" that may be exaggerated to the point of literalness and narrowness.[2]

We will see that these traits of making others comfortable and wanting to be comfortable themselves directly reflect the idealized essential quality. It is no wonder that the Enneagram of idealizations succinctly describes the Nine's ego ideal as "I am comfortable." In fact, all Nine traits—not asserting oneself and not confronting, keeping things harmonious, being good mediators, and so on—are limited reflections of this orientation to comfort and help form the Nine's ego ideal.

It is amazing how the traits of Nines basically result from what is a little twist in their understanding of this essential quality. Most Nines are not far off from this quality, yet this little twist actually alienates them in a deep way from their essential being. We can say that the Nine's traits are an approximation of the apparent characteristics of this quality. But an approximation of characteristics, regardless of how close, cannot connect us with the actual presence. It does not make the mentally constructed personality and belief system become essential being. Nines are, in fact, forgetful of their essential being, heedless about what matters most, and their close approximations simply distance them from the truth and keep them asleep to their true condition, their true being, and to the very fact that they are asleep. Hence their numbness and superficiality. But the ones who wake up to the fact that they are asleep tend to be great seekers of reality and truth. And their realization translates itself into essential or significant action. A good example of this is Paramahansa Yogananda, as we see in his book *Autobiography of a Yogi*.

Hudson and Riso write the following:

> Nines demonstrate the universal temptation to ignore the disturbing aspects of life and to seek some degree of peace and comfort by numbing out. They respond to pain and suffering by attempting to live in a state of premature peacefulness, whether it is in a state of false spiritual attainment or in a more gross denial. More than any other type, Nines demonstrate the tendency to run away from the paradoxes and tensions of life by attempting to transcend them or by seeking simple and painless solutions to their problems.[3]

These traits express the seeking for the idealized essential quality, as many of the things Nines want in their life are reflections of the true characteristics of this quality of being. It is understandable and natural that people want less discord—they want peace, harmony, and security in their lives. But the real way to attain these qualities is through being grounded in reality, with eyes wide open. These qualities happen as a result of grappling with pain and difficulties, not by closing one's eyes to the suffering and discord that tend to permeate society and characterize human life on this earth.

THE IDEALIZED ASPECT:
BOUNDLESS LOVE

There are two primary steps to waking up from sleep. First, we must wake up to our actual present condition of being fixated and asleep. This is what Gurdjieff referred to as "the terror of the moment." This means that when we learn about our type, we do not take it merely as typology. Nor is it like tea leaves or something written in the stars. We do not have to be this way. In fact, the fixations simply refer to the structured and limited consciousness that we have come to believe we are. To take the first step of waking up is to recognize the fixations as fixations—rigid, learned traits and dynamics that we can be free from and rise above by realizing what we have been truly seeking without knowing it. Second is to wake up to reality, to what we are and to the nature of the reality that we live in.

The quality that arises to help us in our awakening is boundless love. It takes us from the individual level of spirituality to the boundless and nondual realms. We can say it is the beginning and, in fact, the best entrance into nondual realization. Because it is a ground of nondual presence, it is, in some sense, the source of all qualities and diamond vehicles. When we experience this nondual dimension, we experience everything, including the relative level of experience and essential qualities, as made out of love.

Because nondual realization is universal and all-pervasive, when Nines seek peace, they unconsciously do so not only for themselves but for others as well. So, they work to eliminate discord in their lives and also in the lives of others by being good mediators and peacemakers. Their attempt to avoid the negative, and their desire to feel good and without discord, is a reflection of this selfless and encompassing love. For in this quality, there is only goodness, goodness everywhere pervading everything. More accurately, this quality offers us the potential of recognizing that all reality can be seen as good or that there is the potentiality of true goodness everywhere.

This perspective does not align with some of the nondual traditions, like some branches of Advaita Vedanta. This would be somewhat similar on a different level to falling into the trap of the Nine: denying true suffering and the real difficulties of the world. The world is real, and its difficulties do not go away through nondual realization. Grappling with those difficulties directly using the wisdom of nonduality is an important way to achieve some freedom and relief from them. And perhaps help free others from some of their personal or cultural suffering. Yet, the ordinary world remains and continues to follow the laws of physics. The teaching of the Diamond Approach recognizes the ordinary world as a potential of Being and not simply an illusion.

The natural endowment of type Nine is this boundless or divine love, but it is also universal consciousness or cosmic light. It has to do with awakening, being open-eyed and directly conscious of what is possible in the spiritual realm. It is about becoming conscious of this realm and inviting it to pervade and fill our lives and the lives of others with its goodness, light, and freedom. This helps us understand the traits of peacemaker and mediator. A true peacemaker brings harmony to the world, something that makes sense and becomes possible with the realization of divine love—when we have integrated the spiritual realm and its treasures of luminosity, love, and wisdom.

Nines want to bring peace by avoiding conflict and difficulty. The quality of divine love makes it possible to bring peace, meaning, and harmony, but only by confronting the difficulty. It is not the quality that is needed in actually confronting and grappling with the conflicts and difficulties. For this we need essential strength and will, along with essential intelligence and compassion. However, the quality of divine love gives us a basic sense of trust, a feeling of being held by a benevolent presence that comforts and soothes. It is actually what is needed on the spiritual path at times of difficult transitions, such as big losses or fragmentation. These are often times of trial, fear, or challenge. Boundless love is what allows the seeker to feel trusting enough to deal with the situation and to move on to other as yet unknown dimensions. It can work similarly in dealing with difficulties of the world and of our ongoing life as well. It grants us trust and ease, which make it possible for us to harness other essential qualities that ensure that the mediation or peacemaking is real and effective. I have referred to it as loving light or living daylight in my book *Facets of Unity*.[4]

PRESENCE OF BOUNDLESS LOVE

This love is not like the essential quality of merging gold love that Twos idealize. The merging gold love is more relational and more relevant for connection, unity, and sharing, as well as community and intimacy. This love feels different, with a different texture and taste, a different color and function. Yet both are love. In some sense, boundless love is more fundamental than merging gold love. It is the sea of love that differentiates itself into many kinds of love that are relevant for human beings and their lives. Before we encounter the nondual way of experiencing this quality, it appears as a pervasive loving light, as the delicate presence of a love that is not separate from consciousness. We feel held or bathed by a softness all around us that infuses the whole atmosphere. We feel soothed, comforted, and trusting, making it easy to relax and let go. When this quality is present in our consciousness, the sense of ease and relaxation feels completely natural.

Some people experience boundless love as arising within them, as loving light, as a softness that is a delicate presence. It feels like a golden white presence, soft and sweet, but not as intensely sweet as merging love. When it arises within, it is relaxing and brings an inner ease and a settling of mind and consciousness. While we experience it as love, we see it as light, a field of yellowish-white light, a delicate presence with a soft, delicate substantiality. In that quality of light, we recognize it is conscious of itself—pure consciousness that is awake and conscious of its nature.

Others first experience it as arising around them in the environment. It bathes them, holds, caresses, and soothes them, as if a tender loving hand is touching them in a way that makes them feel love is present. This evokes a profound sense of holding that makes it easy for them to relax and surrender.

Of course, others can experience this love-consciousness as both inside and outside, permeating and suffusing everything. When we are still experiencing ourselves as autonomous individuals, boundless love feels boundless and pervasive but not yet the nature of everything. It is similar to how most people experience inner space at the beginning of the inner journey; like physical space, it is everywhere, yet it is also separate from everything.

The deeper experience of this quality of consciousness takes us to a boundless condition. The love is pervasive and boundless as stated, but now it penetrates everything so explicitly that nothing is outside of it. This makes us feel that, since it fills everything to its deepest and furthest regions, it is not separate from any part of reality. We feel a medium—an expansive, infinite continuum of consciousness and love—that not only bathes, holds, and fills us but is our very nature. It is what we are, whether we are experiencing ourselves as body or soul. Therefore, we recognize this love and consciousness not only as a quality that arises locally but also as infinite, without boundaries—hence, we refer to it as a boundless dimension. Its absence of boundaries means that not even our skin or our atoms can bound it or keep it out; nothing keeps it out. It penetrates everything so thoroughly that everything is made of it. Thus we have arrived at divine love, which is the source or origin of the quality of loving light or boundless love as experienced by the individual soul.

Divine love is like loving light and has many of its characteristics, but it has more body, more texture. It is still soft but in a heavenly and blissful way. It is not only comforting, it is goodness itself, pure unadulterated love of the divine. Some might connect it to a deity or to God, but we can also experience it simply as the matrix we come from, our origin and nature. As this realization deepens, we experience ourselves as a boundless field of beautiful, luminous, lightly golden, sweet love. And because of this, we feel connected to everything through this conscious love, so connected that we may realize we are everything. As the experience continues to open, we can recognize ourselves as this infinite field in more than four dimensions, a boundless presence that is the nature and the composition of everything—we are everything. This is likely the most well-known mystical experience of oneness or unity. In the East, it is referred to as nondual reality.

Divine love brings in the oneness of everything, which is the entry into the nondual realm of experience. The nondual is not only love; it is also consciousness, presence, awareness, and emptiness. But love reveals the pure goodness we can experience, that our spiritual nature is good in the way pure, giving, generous, selfless love is good. This dimension reveals the beauty and goodness, the blissfulness and color, the richness and holding of the spiritual universe.

CHARACTERISTICS
OF BOUNDLESS LOVE

Nines do not need to experience boundless love on this level of divine love to be liberated from the confines of their fixation. Experiencing and integrating its expression as loving light impacting the individual soul will be quite sufficient to reveal what they are after. It is much easier to experience loving light than divine love, for the latter requires the transition from ordinary to nondual experiencing. Once Nines integrate boundless love as loving light, they can recognize many of their patterns as attempts to express or seek this quality of their true being.

The movement toward no conflict and no confrontation is a reflection of the action of loving light. It makes things easy and relaxes whatever the situation is so that action can simply arise and express itself. There is no avoidance or denial of difficulty in this process. Loving light simply holds the situation in a loving way so that the basic trust that comes from this quality provides the ground needed to deal with that situation. When we feel loving light, we feel it is easier to deal with whatever the difficulty or conflict is. It is not exactly confidence, which arises from will. It is a trust that things will work out. This is one of the characteristics, or functions, of this essential quality. It is a love that holds and embraces the soul so that it feels tranquil and comfortable, even at times of challenge and conflict.

We can understand now the seeking of the Nine for comfort, peace, and the absence of challenge. This presence is a real expression of the consciousness that makes even the body feel relaxed and at ease. Everything feels as if it goes smoothly and effortlessly, and the more we embody this quality, the more smoothly and effortlessly things go in our lives. There is actually, then, less strife.

Even when there is conflict or threat, we feel the inner relaxation necessary to allow us to clearly discern what is happening, which in turn allows the other essential qualities to arise, offering their capacities for courage, intelligence, confidence, and so on. The state of ease allows the soul to open to its inner capacities, which can then aid it in dealing with the difficulties of life. The result is a kind of comfort that is more a freedom from concern and anxiety, with an inner ease that makes us feel settled.

Since we are inwardly at peace, the need to look for distractions in the external and unessential dissolves. The peace is not outward, though this inner peace can radiate out to give us external peace as well. We don't look for distractions because this quality expresses divine love, which is the richness, wonder, and beauty of reality. Why would we look outside for little things and collect more items than we need when inwardly we feel in touch with a deep richness and behold everything as glimmering with beauty? Not to mention the affect of pure bliss that is soft and flowing, sweet and giving. Nines can then become naturally generous, for they are overflowing with selfless love and goodness. They do not need to idealize generosity, for generosity is the natural characteristic of this quality. Its presence in the soul causes Nines to become generous with their being, not just with things and actions.

Real action replaces the busy kind of activity in which Nines engage. We see that this busy activity is a distortion of real essential action. Liberated Nines can now take real action to bring peace and harmony, for they come from the harmony of divine love and its boundless goodness. They can use their essential strength, will, intelligence and effectiveness to attend to the difficulties and issues—their personal ones and collective ones—in order to bring a true resolution and connectedness. The inner unity can express itself as the movement and drive toward outer tolerance, cooperation, appreciation, and inclusivity. Nines are no longer involved in the distractions of the peripheral and superficial and now focus more on the essential and necessary. This is the action of the liberated Nine. A good exemplar of the liberated Nine might be Oscar Ichazo. It's quite likely that he is a Nine, as he demonstrates many of these qualities. He worked diligently for many decades to establish the Arica School and develop a new multifaceted teaching based on the Enneagram. And he used "Humanity Is Only One Spirit" as the motto for his school.

We see how closely the Nine traits and patterns resemble the characteristics of their essential endowment, but also how far they are from the real. When Nines see that these patterns are due to a kind of idealized picture of how they want to be, that there is an ego ideal they hold, the rigidity of these traits will begin to soften. Recognizing the ego ideal, which includes generosity, peacemaking, comfort, and harmony, is a good beginning. Understanding that this is a constructed picture in their minds that might reflect a deeper intuition opens them to being affected by the real quality. When Nines recognize and see the ego ideal as an ego ideal, they come even closer to presence. By letting go of the ideal, not identifying with it, and especially recognizing that it is an imitation or approximation of something real, this quality of realness may find the opening to arise for them.

THE DIRECT APPROACH
TO BOUNDLESS LOVE

Exposing the ideal is a gradual, though indirect, approach. It is easier and more direct to simply recognize the lack of trust Nines have—their insecurity and fear of conflict and confrontation—as patterns that can be worked through and not inborn characteristics of themselves. By understanding the absence of this basic trust and the lack of loving holding that they seek, and by not trying to find comfort or peace, they may begin to feel the actual absence of the essential quality. The Enneagram of avoidances succinctly identifies that what they avoid most is "conflict." Other ways they may tap into the absence of the quality are to feel the inner deficiency as a feeling of being disconnected from the ground of Being or of not ever being held adequately or as the lack of the feeling of selfless generosity. It can feel like a painful absence of loving holding, which is usually an aching, even scary, emotional and existential state.

It is frequently the case that negative feelings about God or spiritual reality will surface. This could be cynicism or outright rage and anger at God. It is necessary to deal with this hatred and its sources in one's history and one's belief system about reality in order to open up to the arising of loving light.[5]

If Nines can remain with this deficiency and lack, not fighting it, denying it, or distracting themselves from it, it can become the empty space where the boundless love emerges and bathes them with its blessing of softness. It might emerge within them or outside as an embracing soft presence, as if the universe is a loving and caring mother. By experiencing and integrating this essential quality and recognizing it as a quality of their nature, Nines may see their patterns begin to reveal themselves as historical distortions and impressions. If Nines—or any of us—are lucky or prepared enough to experience divine love itself, then it becomes a nondual awakening to reality, where we experience the unity of being as love and goodness.

10

Point Five
DIAMOND GUIDANCE

The primary defenses of type Five are avoidance and emotional distancing, which led Ichazo to refer to them as Ego-Stinge, for withholding emotional connection. Their ego ideal is related to knowledge and understanding, learning and figuring things out. They may idealize knowledge and its accumulation, but it is usually in the service of understanding. Riso and Hudson write the following:

> We have named personality type Five the *Investigator* because, more than any other type, Fives want to find out why things are the way they are. They want to understand how the world works, whether it is the cosmos, the microscopic world, the animal, vegetable, or mineral kingdom—or the inner world of imagination. They are always searching, asking questions, and delving into things in depth.[1]

Since the idealization is a reflection of an essential quality, the knowledge and understanding they value is mental rather than essential. The Enneagram of idealizations offers two phrases to express the ego ideal of the Five: "I know" and "I am full." Since Fives place so much importance on knowing, it is logical that emotional detachment would become part of the idealization. This can make them loners who prize privacy and conceptual learning over social relating. Sandra Maitri writes the following:

> What a Five feels she lacks and believes she needs is more knowledge and understanding. This makes sense, since if you take the stance of an onlooker at life, knowing what is going on becomes central to your very sense of survival.[2]

For Fives, knowledge represents nourishment that they feel they lack. They are constantly trying to fill this underlying emptiness of disconnection with more knowledge. However, it is an emptiness that can never be filled in this way.

Thus, all of these elements—the knower, the detached observer, the one who understands and investigates—are part of their ego ideal. We will see how these are related to their idealized quality, and how the characteristics of this quality help us understand the patterns and dynamics of their shell. Naranjo gives us another flavor of the same dynamic for type Five:

> One psychodynamic consequence of this existential pain of feeling faintly existing is the attempt to compensate for the impoverishment of feeling and active life through the intellectual life (for which the individual is usually well endowed constitutionally) and through being a curious and/or critical "outsider."[3]

Naranjo is a good example of the intellectual type, which is obvious from the many areas he wrote about. But he was a more developed Five, for he delved into the investigation of the spiritual realm and practiced many teachings and became a teacher himself. Yet, he retained the emotional detachment and the relational withdrawal tendency that characterizes the type. Other examples include Supreme Court Justice Ruth Bader Ginsburg and poet Emily Dickinson.

THE IDEALIZED ASPECT: DIAMOND GUIDANCE

To understand the Five ego ideal that patterns the external part of the fixation (that is, the shell, not its core), we need to have some understanding of the idealized spiritual quality. We arrive here, as we did for type Seven, at another diamond vehicle. For type Seven the idealized quality was associated with the Markabah, the pleasure vehicle, domain of essential pleasure. We saw that it had all the various essential qualities but in a particular configuration and in a form where each quality was a different kind of pleasure. So, kindness is experienced as pleasure, intelligence is experienced as pleasure, and so on. Though each feels and tastes differently, the vehicle encompasses all of them. For type Five, we refer to the manifestation of our spiritual or essential nature as the diamond guidance or "nous." Diamond guidance refers to our essential intellect. Ordinary intellect is but a reflection of essential intellect since it is not connected to our true nature. This manifestation of our spiritual or true nature is not that well known or documented. It is rare to find somebody who actually knows essential intellect in its specificity and its functionality, and who embodies it in such a way that it expresses itself in their life. Idries Shah, the late Sufi teacher, used it well, but he was a Three, not a Five. The Dalai Lama also embodies this diamond guidance, but he is again most likely not a Five.

In our times, when we refer to intellect, we are considering only the ordinary intellect that employs thinking and remembering to understand a situation or a problem. It might surprise many to know, then, that ancient Greeks understood there were many levels of intellect, ranging from the ordinary mental intellect that most people use to the essential and divine intellects, with many refinements in between. But even the most advanced teaching traditions, such as Tibetan Buddhism, Vedanta, and Kabbalah, do not have a clear understanding of what I refer to as diamond guidance. Some teachers of these paths seem to have realized essential intellect, as in the case of the Dalai Lama and the late Idries Shah. However, I don't see many current teachers who embody it or know it.

Most people, including most spiritual teachers, consider intellect to be only mental, part of the ordinary mental apparatus. Yet, essential intellect can be the most useful way of understanding our spiritual experience and even our ordinary experience. Krishnamurti had a partial embodiment of it, but he was a Six, not a Five. Diamond guidance could function through him but only with knowledge of the present moment; he could not use data from the past to help his understanding of what was going on. Krishnamurti, along with most other such teachers, subscribed to the view that mind and intellect are impediments to spiritual experience and awakening. This can definitely be true, but only if one is functioning at the level of the ordinary mind or mental intellect. If we know what the diamond guidance is, we will first be surprised, then amazed, and finally incredulous at such an elegant appearance of our true nature. We can see how skillful it is in guiding our experience and understanding out of the morass of ego and fixated experience and into the land of truth, to the realm of pure spirit. Diamond guidance is actually the messenger of spirit, the discerning instrument of our true nature. It is the closest thing in our teaching to the Holy Spirit of Christianity.

Diamond guidance is unexpected in its truth and presence and mysterious in how it functions in guiding our investigation and exploration of the truth of experience. In its full realization it guides and helps at all levels of experience, from the ordinary ego level to the various spiritual levels of experience and realization. It has the uncanny capacity to combine the data of our experience in the here and now with data and knowledge from the past, i.e., learned knowledge. It can take our remembered knowledge, whether from experience or study, and discern what is relevant from it for our present experience, explicating the meaning of the experience in the here and now. Therefore, our understanding and appreciation of the meaning of what is happening now is more complete, for it includes the wisdom of all times.

This runs counter to the customary spiritual wisdom that says the mind and intellect are impediments to spiritual experience. In fact, it is not possible to have a complete and precise understanding of our spiritual experience and realization without some realization of this level of intellect—the intellect of light and luminous presence. It discerns, synthesizes, and brings about an experiential comprehension of our experience, whether ordinary or spiritual, thus opening the door to further spiritual discoveries and evolution. It develops the capacity for critical thinking on the spiritual level, so even spiritual realization does not escape this most exacting critical thinking imbued by light and wisdom. It is the true guide on the spiritual journey, which is why in the Diamond Approach we call it diamond guidance. It is a diamond vehicle, so it has all qualities, each as an expression of essential clarity, but all configured in such a way that works to recognize and discern the truth of any experience or manifestation.

PRESENCE OF DIAMOND GUIDANCE

I remember the first time I encountered this presence in a full and complete way. Before this, I had only experienced it as a delicate throbbing presence at the center of my forehead, its main place of operation, as I describe in some detail in my book *Luminous Night's Journey*. That day, I was with a couple of friends discussing the throbbing presence, attempting to recognize what it was and what it was for. As we discussed the experience and how it was occurring, we felt the atmosphere in the room change—as if being charged by something subtle yet powerful. All of us felt a presence descending into the room—or emerging in the space—that was of a different order than any quality we had experienced before. I felt a sense of sacredness—that we were in the presence of the sacred. At first the space in the room felt peaceful and settled, transparent, with a stillness to it. In this sacred space appeared a vehicle of variegated colors, a form of presence so delicate, while at the same time powerful and impactful. The whole room was filled by this sacred, refined, and transparent form of presence comprised of luminous colored diamonds. Each diamond was the diamond form of an essential quality, and all essential qualities were present in this form of transparent limpid diamonds—each one a different color of clarity. It was as though clarity differentiated itself into many transparent but totally clean and precise presences. At the same time they were all part of the same presence, configured to form one manifestation with its own functionality and wisdom. I felt transported, delighted, and totally clear. The perception and the experience were clear-cut and diamond-like in the sharpness of their precision. The perception was precise and clear, the experience was precise and clear, and the mental functioning was precise and clear. The feeling was that we were visited by a divine emissary, a messenger from the transcendent. Later on, we understood it as equivalent to the angel of revelation in the monotheistic traditions. Sometimes this angel is referred to as Gabriel, as in Gabriel who revealed the sacred to Mohammad. The Sufis sometimes refer to Khidr, or the green guide, and the Kabbalah refers to Izayah.

The mental functioning was not just mental anymore. It used thoughts and images but also feelings and memories—at the same time as it included direct knowing of what was there—to form a whole picture of what was happening in the here and now. It took us a while to recognize it as the instrument for essential understanding. All spiritual paths assert that we need to understand our experience for true and full realization to occur, that experience by itself is not enough. Experience and understanding the experience without being separate from it is the full and complete awakening or realization. It turned out that we had been gifted this most precious of essential manifestations, the guide to truth and enlightenment—intellect on the essential level. From that place, it was easy to see that our usual intellect is a pale reflection of this true sacred intellect. We also recognized that when different teachings tell us to drop the mind, they mean drop the ordinary mind, not the essential intellect. For many of them utilize this manifestation, whether they discriminate it in their experience or not.

Diamond guidance has no size. In this experience it filled the whole room, but it can expand endlessly, pervading the whole universe. However, its most common way of appearing is as a small (perhaps two inches wide) diamond presence of clarity and wisdom. It can move around our body and our consciousness, illuminating an area and revealing its true objective, as opposed to subjective, meaning. The most common way this guidance operates is to reside at the center of the forehead as a delicate throbbing presence, shiny and luminous, the way it initially did for me. It operates in the black latifa center of the Sufi system, the latifa they call *khafi*, or "hidden." It combines the heart and the mind in its functioning as the essential intellect, the discerning intelligence of Being. It is equivalent to what the Buddhists call Manjushri, for Manjushri is the bodhisattva of wisdom and discerning intelligence. This is one of the major essential manifestations in Buddhism, like Avalokiteshvara, the bodhisattva of compassionate action.

CHARACTERISTICS OF DIAMOND GUIDANCE

Diamond guidance is the only essential manifestation I know of that can combine ordinary knowledge from study and previous experience with direct spiritual experience, called gnosis. Hence, its utility extends beyond simple experience and awakening. It turns out to be the authentic guide of our true being, as well as the discerning spiritual intelligence that combines ordinary intelligence with the presence of our true being. Fives idealize this manifestation of Being because it is their natural spiritual endowment, and they have some intuitive, vague sense of it. However, usually they neither know it for what it is, nor anticipate such a reality. So, the ego ideal becomes a distant reflection of this presence, which is distorted depending on how disconnected the particular Five is from it. Fives tend to idealize knowledge and ways of accessing knowledge. But they do not know that the true intellect functions by synthesizing data from the past with direct mystical knowing in the present. As a result they think intellect consists of ordinary bits of knowledge—data collected from observation, study, and books—arranged in logical and insightful ways. Hence their desire to collect knowledge and to understand its meaning.

Fives become knowers, but because their knowledge is only intellectual, mental, and cerebral, it disconnects them further from true intellect, which is a presence of Being. As Hudson wrote, Fives want to understand, but since they only have a vague sense of what true, full understanding is, their understanding becomes a deduction from ordinary mental knowledge or a synthesis of external observations of nature. This kind of intellectual or mental understanding is useful for practical living, scientific research, and all kinds of study, but it falls short for the study of spiritual experience and the spiritual realm. Spiritual understanding is the understanding of true nature, the true presence of our being, and what we awaken to in spiritual realization. In addition, diamond guidance is the discerning intelligence and synthesizing intellect that can help us understand any experience, from the past or present, ordinary or spiritual. As such, it is an understanding that always leads to spiritual illumination. It can start with ordinary mental or emotional experience, but it ends up opening us to the spiritual dimension. This guidance can lead us all the way to awakening and enlightenment.

Like all of us, Fives want enlightenment. But before they become aware of the spiritual origins of this drive, they think of it as the illumination of natural phenomena, of the mind, or of human psychology. They pursue many areas of knowledge—scientific, literary, or artistic—and can excel in all areas of this kind of understanding, as exemplified by Sigmund Freud and Hermann Hesse. But if Fives are able to explore the spiritual dimensions of knowing, they can arrive at true illumination, which is spiritual awakening. This was the case for the Buddha, who is considered to have been a Five type.

Part of the functioning of essential intelligence is direct and precise perception of what is going on. Perception is the function of consciousness, and spiritual perception is the function of pure consciousness. Perception for essential intellect, however, is not simply perception but clear and precise perception. Precision is an important feature of the functioning of this presence. The reflection of this capacity is to be as good an observer as possible. Fives excel at being observers but only from a distance and without getting involved. They idealize detached and distant observation, which is necessary for science but not for spiritual experiencing and understanding.

For Fives, this can manifest as isolation that results from being emotionally detached or distant from their emotional life. This is, of course, a distorted imitation of one way that essential intellect functions—it observes in a way that generates objective knowledge. Objective knowledge means that it is not under the sway of our beliefs and ideas or the influences of time. For knowledge to be the truth of the situation as it is, it cannot be contaminated by our mental positions and theories, for it is a completely open and neutral understanding. However, this does not happen by distancing ourselves from our emotional life. We need to feel our emotions fully to be able to understand them and their influence on our observations and knowledge. The inner endeavor is to understand ourselves as deeply as possible, and this can only happen if we welcome all of our experience, in all of its dimensions. This includes the mental but also the emotional and, most importantly, the spiritual. Such understanding is what opens up the soul to further illumination and spiritual awakening.

Since Fives idealize the quality of objective experience without knowing what it is, it becomes distorted as distancing from experience in general, especially from emotional experience. The distancing satisfies the scientific method and the idealization of knowledge but also fuels the Five's defense of avoiding difficult emotions and life situations. Consequently, they become isolated from their direct experience, which ordinarily is the basis of the emotional and relational life of human beings, and so, at times, Fives turn into loners.

While Fives' appreciation for objectivity and noninterference with the observed can make them great scientists, as in the case of the greatest mathematician of the twentieth century, Kurt Gödel, this is not what is needed for understanding oneself. To unravel our fixation and penetrate its core, we must look inward, first to our mind and heart, then deeper still into our soul and, finally, all the way to our spiritual core. Diamond guidance can aid us in truly, objectively understanding the Five shell and its patterns, for it not only reveals and fully understands the psychological origins of those patterns from past experiences, but it does so with spiritual illumination and the immediacy of presence.

When the essential intellect is operating in this mode, it is usually felt at the center of the forehead with a sense that there is an actual presence of something true and real, a source of light and illuminating understanding. The understanding is then experiential and direct, and it includes the mind without being simply mental, or patterned by mental knowledge. What a blessing for a spiritual seeker to have such an essential support on the spiritual path, as well as for enlightened living!

When the diamond guidance operates in the center of the forehead, the blue and green essential qualities tend to be dominant, along with the solid gold. Solid gold represents truth, the truth of the moment that eventually extends all the way to ultimate truth. Blue signifies an essential quality we have not discussed yet. It is the quality that has to do with spiritual knowing, which is direct knowing—gnosis or *jnana*. Gnosis means the knowing is immediate, where the known, the knower, and the knowledge are one thing—a total nonduality of knowledge. This capacity for knowing, whose center is located in the pineal gland at the center of the brain, becomes possible when the blue aspect is integrated. It unifies the right and left hemispheres of the brain, and its presence calms the mind, leaving it carefree and open to new and unexpected knowing. It is the knowing of Being manifesting specifically as a particular quality of presence. It is delicate and subtle, and blissful in its quietness. It silences the thinking mind, allowing for the emergence of spiritual experience, and then the understanding of that experience with the totality of the essential intellect.

The green quality represents the heart and the heart center, especially the attuned kindness of the heart. It is soft, tender, and warm, and it opens the heart to all of its content, helping us welcome in our difficult experiences and any suffering that may come with them. That is why the doorway to this quality of presence is tolerating emotional hurt and wounding without avoidance, distance, schizoid defenses, or detachment. It is welcoming our wounds in a way that allows this green empathic presence to arise and heal the wound. This compassionate capacity to welcome and tolerate suffering becomes necessary for seeing the truth of our experience. We cannot know or understand our ultimate truth in any completeness without first experiencing and understanding our relative, mostly emotional, and relational truth. Since relative truth tends to involve much pain and suffering, the green presence is essential for opening to that truth. Essential understanding is a matter of first understanding the true meaning of our experience, then diving more deeply into experientially understanding our spiritual truth. That is why realization is referred to as awakening, for it is experience that is inseparable from insight into the experience.

Fives love insights, but as we have seen, such insights are largely mental, being the product of ordinary intellect. This works fine for many areas of life, especially the scientific fields. However, for insights into our true nature we need a more encompassing intellect, that of diamond guidance, which uses all the qualities of essence in its function of illumination and comprehension. The comprehension then is of experience and ultimately of our true being.

By observing and recognizing the idealization of knowledge and understanding, objectivity and observation, the Five can penetrate to essential intellect. But for this to happen the Five needs to first understand and appreciate that the idealization is a reflection, an approximation, and, in fact, a distorted approximation. This leaves the Five in a state of not knowing for a while. This peaceful not knowing, if welcomed, can become the open space within which the essential intellect emerges with its scintillating lights.

THE DIRECT APPROACH
TO DIAMOND GUIDANCE

As with the other Enneatypes, there is a more direct way of accessing essential intellect. This is by first allowing ourselves to not know and to see that not knowing is not only true but peaceful and quiet. By recognizing that we do not know how to understand our experience directly—especially by recognizing that we can have spiritual experience but still find it difficult to have insight into it—we become primed for the emergence of this true emissary of truth. We must also see through our position that knowing and understanding are only mental, otherwise it may obstruct the arising of this presence.

Fives tend to avoid "emptiness," according to the Enneagram of avoidances. But emptiness will arise as we see the mental knowledge we have accumulated as abstract and lifeless, which is what knowledge is when acquired without being in touch with one's feelings, as a product of a schizoid defense. Also, by seeing that our clarity is only clarity of thinking, not a state of clarity, we can be prepared for this essential vehicle, which has the clarity of presence. In this state of clarity, the medium of presence is transparent and clear. Essential intellect is an embodiment of this clarity but utilizes all qualities as forms of clarity. Recognizing the absence or ignorance of this capacity can open us up to a barren emptiness, a lack that when allowed brings a new possibility. This is the diamond guidance arising with its exquisite presence and subtle lights of spiritual illumination. It is both a presence and an instrument of understanding at all levels of being.

It also helps to inquire into our capacities for analysis and synthesis and to see the way they are limited to the external and the mental. Understanding utilizes analysis and synthesis, but our ordinary intellect does this with ordinary data, not with experience, and especially not with immediate experience. Many spiritual practitioners are afraid of understanding their spiritual experience because they fear that would indicate the presence of the thinking mind, which would cut them off from their spiritual presence. Thinking mind certainly does this, but it is still possible to study our spiritual experience and analyze its characteristics. Remember, the diamond guidance includes the aspect of brilliancy and through its analysis, a synthesis can arise naturally and spontaneously as insight, without relying on mental deduction. We need to be open to the possibility of higher intellect and realize that when spiritual teachings tell us to drop the mind, they are referring to the thinking intellectual mind, not to all knowing and understanding.

Through awakening the essential intellect, Fives are liberated from the limited mental perspective that dominates the shell and this open-mindedness and direct knowing is vital to help penetrate the core of their fixation. But all types will benefit from access to the diamond guidance—synthesizing what is known and penetrating what is unknown as it provides understanding and insight for the soul's journey toward liberation.

AFTERWORD

To really make use of the material you've just finished reading, it needs to be moved out of the conceptual realm and become experiential. That's the only way that the keys Almaas is offering will indeed become transformative.

The material in this book is the product of over fifty years of in-depth inner exploration both personally and with Almaas's students. Such sincere inner engagement is what it takes to truly understand the territory that the map of the Enneagram charts. Otherwise, it remains simply information—albeit fascinating information. It's only in the past forty-five years or so that the Enneagram has been taught on its own, outside of the context of spiritual endeavor.

It was in the context of deep inner work that Almaas and I both learned the Enneagram, and it is still the context in which we teach it in the work of the Diamond Approach, the spiritual path that came through and has been developed by Almaas. We learned the Enneagram as part of the pioneering SAT work founded by Claudio Naranjo in which he utilized psychological tools to facilitate and support spiritual work. It was the primary psychological tool that he taught. Almaas has carried on that orientation of working with our psychology to loosen up our ego structure, making access to our deepest nature more possible. And he has dramatically expanded upon the use of the Enneagram.

One of the biggest discoveries Almaas made is the differentiations of the divine or true nature. He saw first of all that our deepest nature in all its manifestations is characterized by presence—that it is substantial, palpable, and immediate. And he saw that our nature is not static—it is not always experienced as love or emptiness or pure awareness or any of the other ways our fundamental nature is described in the various traditions. It manifests in different forms at different times in our lives and at different stages of spiritual development. Additionally, he observed that each differentiation of true nature is obscured by specific sectors of our ego or personality structure. Working with those sectors, he discovered, allows access and stabilization of access to each of these qualities of Being. He also discovered that there is a typical order of access to particular qualities and their associated issues when we take a deep inner dive, and this has become the logos or overarching framework of the teaching Almaas developed.

He discovered that the absence of contact with true nature in the various ways it arises leaves empty places in our consciousness. That absence is covered over and compensated for with various defenses and structures of the personality. Instead of transcending these manifestations of our egoic structure as the classical spiritual traditions have attempted to do, he realized that by penetrating them through experiential contact and exploration, they would relax in time. Then they would reveal the empty places or holes they fill and obscure. These holes lead us to believe that something is missing in us—that something is deficient about us—and experientially these holes can feel like parts of our body are missing. In reality, what's missing is *contact* with the various qualities of our deepest nature.

Almaas found that if we truly allow the experience of the holes and experientially jump inside of them (instead of over them), something miraculous happens: the quality of true nature missing from our conscious awareness will emerge. This perception forms the basis of the methodology of the Diamond Approach. We are learning to become fully present and to experientially explore what we find in our living consciousness. Whether what's here is egoic in nature or a particular state of Being, whatever it is will inevitably open up and reveal a deeper dimension of truth. In working with ourselves in this way, our process deepens, and who and what we know ourselves to be transforms over time. We gradually access and then embody true nature, becoming humans who link the invisible realms with the physical.

In addition to developing a new form of spiritual technology, Almaas has made significant contributions to deepening the understanding of the Enneagram. *Facets of Unity*, which was published over twenty years ago, filled out the meaning of the holy ideas. We had learned about these nine enlightened views of reality from Naranjo, but the teaching about them was skeletal. Almaas's explication brought them to life. He made them accessible to anyone who had done enough inner work to move their understanding beyond the conceptual to the lived experiential.

A few decades ago, Almaas recognized that the traits of each type mimic or attempt to embody specific differentiations of true nature. This is what he has called the "idealized aspect" of each type. This recognition is a point of overlap between the focus of the Diamond Approach on deepening states of consciousness as our work on ourselves unfolds and the original understanding of the traits of the Enneatypes.

He made another discovery about the inner flow, the psychodynamic movement from one point to those following and preceding it along the lines of flow in the map of the Enneagram. He expanded on the theory we learned from Naranjo about the "heart point" of each type—one point back moving against the line of flow from an Enneatype. He realized that the characteristics of each type's heart point describe an inner child suppressed before the age of four. He named this young psychological structure our "soul child," and because it is a deeper structure underneath conditioning of our Enneatype, experientially opening to it brings us closer to ourselves. The idealized aspect of our heart point represents qualities that were part of our expression early on, and so as our access to our soul child deepens, so does our access to this particular quality. Rather than write about the soul child himself, he gave me permission to include this understanding in my first book on the Enneagram, *The Spiritual Dimension of the Enneagram: Nine Faces of the Soul*. Almaas briefly addresses the soul child here in Appendix 1.

In this book, Almaas has fully developed his understanding about the idealized aspects and indicated the link between them and the holy ideas. He shows how the idealized aspects characterize the shell or outer layer of each type and that penetrating the shell allows us to more easily work with the core of each type, the holy ideas, and the tendencies that arise in the wake of their loss.

This penetration allows us to realize experientially the qualities that each Enneatype mimics. But, like everything else on the path, this penetration has to be rooted in our direct experience. Almaas's methodology for this aspect of our journey is that of the Diamond Approach. As he has indicated, the first step to a lived understanding is getting in touch with our bodies. The reason for this is that the different qualities of our deepest nature that are the idealized aspects are only going to be found right here, inside each of us. To find them, or more exactly to open to them, we also have to be right here, present in the immediacy of our experience. This begins with our physical form, our body, because it's only here, in our personal location, that we can know the presence that characterizes these differentiations of our deepest nature.

It's also the place where the patterns that block us from this access are found. While they have emotional and mental components, in the body these patterns appear as tension patterns. Only as these patterns relax through exploring the beliefs, resulting emotions, and physical expression can we contact the presence that we fundamentally are.

Fully landing in our physicality is not easy for most of us unless we have done substantial inner work with that as part of its emphasis. Most people are externally directed, focused on what is going on outside of them and on the content of their minds, rather than on the one who has these experiences. As we learn to tune in to our physical sensations in an ongoing way, we are bypassing our outer and inner content and arriving in the present moment. It's only in the present that we can experience our living consciousness. This cultivation of expanding our attention to include what we are experiencing *and* the one who is experiencing was a fundamental principle in the teaching of the Armenian mystic, G. I. Gurdjieff. And it remains a fundamental principle in the teaching of Almaas.

We also need full access to our emotions. If our emotional life is muted or suppressed, our hearts are not open. An open heart is one of the signs of spiritual development, while a defended heart characterizes entrenchment in our personality structure. As Almaas has shown, some of the most challenging emotions are entryways into the idealized aspects. If we are resistant to experiencing these difficult emotions, like weakness, fear, anger, and hatred, they cannot open up and reveal what qualities of our nature they are masking or distorting.

We also have to confront the places of absence in our psyche, the holes I spoke about earlier. We have seen that each idealized aspect that we are out of touch with results in an absence in the depth of our psyche. Being willing to engage these empty places inside is necessary for them to truly become the portals that they potentially are. Working with our beliefs about what will happen if we go into them and all the forms that our resistance takes allows us to make friends with them—at least enough to let ourselves fully experience them without pulling away. It's only this total allowing, total openness to the experience of our holes, that allows the magic to happen. Like a rabbit emerging from the empty interior of a hat, the missing idealized aspect will naturally manifest, filling our consciousness with its grace.

This is a process we cannot control. A process that we can't manipulate or try to make happen. It requires a real surrender to the empty places inside without expectation. It requires a sincere willingness to find out for ourselves what our inner reality is all about. If you have that kind of sincerity, the keys Almaas has offered here can truly unlock the treasures of your nature.

SANDRA MAITRI

Author of *The Spiritual Dimension of the Enneagram: Nine Faces of the Soul, The Enneagram of Passions and Virtues: Finding the Way Home*, and *When the Heavens Opened*

Appendix 1

ACCESSING
THE SOUL CHILD

We have studied the ego ideal of each fixation from the perspective of the essential aspect or vehicle that it emulates. This is the most effective approach for unlocking the fixation as we have seen. However, for a more complete investigation, we can also study the question of ego ideals in relation to the heart of the fixation.

Enneagram knowledge includes the understanding that each type is connected to the type that represents its heart. The heart of each type is the one that comes before it within the diagrammatic flow of the Enneagram. So, for point Five the heart is Eight, and for point Eight it is Two. The diagrammatic flow proceeds like this: One to Four to Two to Eight to Five to Seven and back to One. The other three types have their own direction within the central triangle. So, what is called the inner movement flows from Nine to Six to Three and back to Nine.

Each type contains its heart as the inner part of its shell. The heart of the shell is the type before it in the inner movement. But what we find quite useful when we study the idealizations is that when we explore each type to find out what that type was like in childhood, generally from ages two to five, they are actually closer to the heart of their eventual type. For example, in childhood the

Two type appears with the qualities and characteristics of the Four. They are more sad and melancholic, wanting to be special but feeling abandoned.

At that age the soul is not yet completely structured as ego, and the fixation has not yet been fully established. (The fixation supposedly becomes set around age seven.) This means that the soul is not fully a personality—not completely mentally structured by ego as in the final type, with a shell patterned by its idealization. Therefore, when we study the type psychodynamically, meaning looking at the underlying forces and structures of childhood, we come upon the child's heart type, before it has settled into ego and its fixation. Since the child is not completely ego at that point, it means the soul is still somewhat active as its living presence—dynamic and alive. The child is a mix at that time of soul dynamic aliveness and ego structures and patterns. This is what we call the soul child, different from what many traditions recognize as the inner child. Because the inner child includes all phases of childhood, it also includes the soul child. But the soul child represents a particular developmental phase of the inner child.

What we find is that the soul child of each type is patterned by the ego ideal of the type before it in the inner movement of the Enneagram. So, type Six's soul child is characterized by the Nine ideal, which is boundless love. Type Seven's soul child is type Five, which is patterned by its idealization of diamond guidance. At this stage, however, it is not just a reflection or imitation of the idealized aspect. Because the soul child is still not completely structured by mind and memory, it is still open to its natural essential endowment. So, the soul child of type Seven is a Five child with the presence of diamond guidance in its experience. It is essential intellect that is mixed with imitations of it and some distortions. Mixed into all of that is the usual conditioning from childhood experience of the child's interactions with their parents or parental figures.

I am bringing in this study of the soul child because it is easier to access the essential quality of the soul child than that of the adult type's shell. It does require the capacity to penetrate the adult fixation in order to access the type's childhood development. But if we access the idealized quality of our soul child, it can help us deal with the adult shell of our own fixation. Let's look at type Five, for example. The Five's soul child is characterized by the Eight type. The Eight's idealized aspect is the strength essence, with its fire and assertion, but it is accompanied by loudness, grossness, and coarse behavior and expression. It hovers between essential presence and ego personality. More accurately, the fire and assertion of the essential presence is imbuing the soul but coming through some of the more structured soul of Eight as coarse and unabashedly loud and assertive. Sometimes, there is anger and strength together. Working with the soul child, there are less fixated structures in the way of experiencing the essential quality. As a result, the essential quality of the soul child is easier to bring forth in service of unraveling one's fixation. For Fives, accessing essential strength makes it easier to work on their adult shell, and in this way they end up realizing their own idealized aspect.

The final result for type Five is to have diamond guidance but also the strength essence. The strength essence will counteract the passivity of the Five, and the essential intellect will replace the ordinary intellect in the Five's study and understanding of self and reality. The two then become important and helpful in penetrating the inner core that is patterned by the loss of access to the holy idea—in this case holy transparency.

This process can reveal how the idealized quality of type Five is related to its holy idea. The holy idea has two facets: holy transparency and holy omniscience. Holy omniscience does not mean knowing everything. Rather, it means the potential capacity to know reality in oneself and in general. Holy omniscience is basically recognizing that all of reality is knowledge, composed of the presence of Being that knows itself everywhere without boundaries. Being manifests reality as the mind of God, where everything is pure mystical knowledge, including not only one's soul but the trees and the mountains and our thoughts. Everything is knowledge and simply knowledge.

Diamond guidance can be seen as related to this cosmic field of knowledge because the holy idea is also holy transparency, which means one is not separate from anything else. All things are nondual with each other, and our individual soul is transparent to all of reality. But when everything is pure knowledge, diamond guidance gives us access to that knowledge—pure spiritual knowledge, with its synthesis of all kinds and levels of knowing.

This is a simple outline of how the idealized quality and the holy idea are related. I am using the Five type to illustrate how the soul child is related to the idealized essential quality and the latter to the holy idea. To go through these elements for all the types would take a whole separate study, which I will not do here. I bring this in briefly for the sake of completeness. The purpose of this book is to learn how to unravel the outer shell of each type by accessing its idealized essential quality. Learning about the essential quality of the soul child can be a valuable tool in this inquiry. Then with all the other tools we have, which are essential qualities, we can penetrate the core of our type and access our holy idea. At that point we are well on our way toward liberation from our fixation—and liberation in general.

Appendix 2
RESOURCES AND REFERENCES

To pursue the personal exploration suggested in this book, you will need some skill in psychological processing, which is part of what we do through the practice of inquiry in the Diamond Approach teaching. The point of learning the principles of this practice is that it reveals more than the workings of our mind and emotions. It enhances psychological processing, transforming it into a spiritual practice that extends our explorations into the spiritual sphere, helping us delve more deeply into our true being, our nature, and its qualities. We are exploring some of the qualities in this book that are relevant to the Enneagram. And all of them are useful in the practice of inquiry, which can loosen the knots of the fixations and their cores.

If you are curious about the practice of inquiry and want to learn more about what is involved, I suggest reading *Spacecruiser Inquiry*, an in-depth and detailed book I wrote about this practice. Another more interactive way of learning inquiry is through online courses offered by our school. You will find these at diamondapproach.org under Online Courses. Currently there is an on-demand course called Discover Your Truth through Diamond Inquiry that is a good introduction to our inquiry practice. There is also Introduction to the Diamond Approach as a general overview of this spiritual path.

The following books by A. H. Almaas are referred to in this book:

Brilliancy: The Essence of Intelligence. Boulder, CO: Shambhala Publications, 2006.

Facets of Unity: The Enneagram of Holy Ideas. Boulder, CO: Shambhala Publications, 1998.

Diamond Heart: Book One: Elements of the Real in Man. Boulder, CO: Shambhala Publications, 1987.

Diamond Heart: Book 5: Inexhaustible Mystery. Boulder, CO: Shambhala Publications, 2011.

Love Unveiled: Discovering the Essence of the Awakened Heart. Boulder, CO: Shambhala Publications, 2020.

The Pearl Beyond Price: Integration of Personality into Being. Boulder, CO: Shambhala Publications, 1988.

The Point of Existence: Transformations of Narcissism in Self-Realization. Boulder, CO: Shambhala Publications, 1996.

Spacecruiser Inquiry: True Guidance for the Inner Journey. Boulder, CO: Shambhala Publications, 2002.

The other books referred to in this book are:

Maitri, Sandra. *The Spiritual Dimension of the Enneagram: Nine Faces of the Soul.* New York, NY: Jeremy Tarcher/Putnam, 2000.

Naranjo, Claudio, M.D. *Ennea-Type Structures: Self-Analysis for the Seeker.* Nevada City, CA: Gateways/IDHHB, Inc., 1991.

Riso, Don Richard, and Russ Hudson. *The Wisdom of the Enneagram: The Complete Guide to Psychological and Spiritual Growth for the Nine Personality Types.* New York, NY: Bantam Books, 1999.

Yogananda, Paramahansa. *Autobiography of a Yogi.* Los Angeles, CA: Self-Realization Fellowship, 2014.

Appendix 3

CHARTS OF THE ENNEAGRAM OF IDEALS AND THE ENNEAGRAM OF AVOIDANCES

ENNEAGRAM OF EGO IDEALS

Comfort/Harmony
9

Strength/ 8
Aggression

1 Perfection/
Rightness

Imagination/ 7
Enjoyment

2 Helpfulness/
Giving

Safety/ 6
Security

3 Success/
Achievement

Knowledge/ 5
Understanding

4 Originality/
Specialness

ENNEAGRAM OF AVOIDANCES

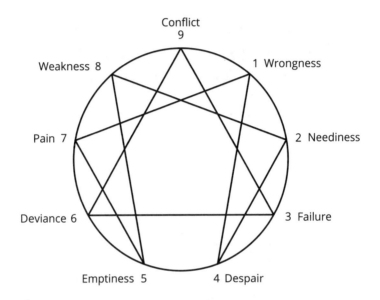

NOTES

POINT EIGHT: TRUE STRENGTH

1. Claudio Naranjo, *Ennea-Type Structures*, 133.

POINT SIX: PERSONAL WILL

1. Naranjo, *Ennea-Type Structures*, 110.

POINT TWO: MERGING LOVE

1. Sandra Maitri, *The Spiritual Dimension of the Enneagram*, 155–56.
2. See my book *Love Unveiled* for more information on the qualities of love.
3. Naranjo, *Ennea-Type Structures*, 45.

POINT ONE: BRILLIANCY

1. Naranjo, *Ennea-Type Structures*, 32.
2. Russ Hudson and Don Riso, *The Wisdom of the Enneagram*, 100.
3. See my book *Brilliancy* for more detail about this aspect and how to access it.

POINT THREE: PERSONAL ESSENCE

1. Naranjo, *Ennea-Type Structures*, 56.
2. Maitri, *Spiritual Dimension of the Enneagram*, 88–89.
3. Hudson and Riso, *Wisdom of the Enneagram*, 153.
4. Refer to my book *The Pearl Beyond Price* for more details and discussion.
5. Refer to *The Pearl Beyond Price*.

POINT FOUR: ESSENTIAL IDENTITY

1. Hudson and Riso, *Wisdom of the Enneagram*, 180.
2. Maitri, *Spiritual Dimension of the Enneagram*, 133.
3. See the work of Heinz Kohut for more information.
4. See my book *The Point of Existence* for more details and discussion.
5. Naranjo, *Ennea-Type Structures*, 79.
6. See my book, *Diamond Heart: Book 5: Inexhaustible Mystery*.
7. The fact that this quality of presence is so central and its realization so difficult is precisely the reason I wrote *The Point of Existence*.

POINT SEVEN: PLEASURE VEHICLE

1. Maitri, *Spiritual Dimension of the Enneagram*, 223.
2. Hudson and Riso, *Wisdom of the Enneagram*, 262.
3. Naranjo, *Ennea-Type Structures*, 123.

POINT NINE: BOUNDLESS LOVE

1. Maitri, *Spiritual Dimension of the Enneagram*, 42–43.
2. Naranjo, *Ennea-Type Structures*, 142.
3. Hudson and Riso, *Wisdom of the Enneagram*, 317.

4. See chapters 5 and 7.

5. For further understanding of the issues arising with boundless love or loving light, refer to chapters 6 and 8 in *Facets of Unity*.

POINT FIVE: DIAMOND GUIDANCE

1. Hudson and Riso, *Wisdom of the Enneagram*, 208.

2. Maitri, *Spiritual Dimension of the Enneagram*, 212.

3. Naranjo, *Ennea-Type Structures*, 89.

INDEX

Elizabeth II, 77
emotions
  access to, 155–56
  in accessing core, 15–16
  capacity to feel, 36–37
  detachment from, 135, 136, 137,
    144–45
  external sources of, 114
  welcoming, 53, 144, 146
emptiness, 105–6, 114
  avoiding, 116
  deficient, 22, 37–38, 54,
    65–66, 78
  of Fives, 136, 147–48
  impersonal, 87
  nondual, 130
  of Sevens, 117, 119–20
  valuing, 93
energy, tantric transformation of,
  34–35, 52
enlightenment, 4, 90, 141, 143
Enneagram, xv
  in Diamond Approach, xxi–
    xxii, 18, 151, 152
  initial work with, 6
  inner engagement needed
    for, 151
  inner flow in, 153–54
  original purpose, 11–12
  popularity of, ix–x
  practice system, xii, xvii, xx
  roots of, xi–xii
  spiritual realization and, 23
  symbol component, xii–xiv,
    xv, xvii

  typology, xii, xiv–xvii, xviii–xx
  in West, 1–2
  See also avoidances,
    Enneagram of; idealizations,
    Enneagram of
Enneatypes, xxiii–xxiv, 1, 16–17,
  22, 145, 153–54. *See also* nine
  types
Enthusiast. *See* Seven (Ego-Plan)
environment, 49, 129
essence, xiii, xx, 53–54. *See also*
  personal essence
Essence (Almaas), xviii
Evagrius of Pontus, xvi, xvii
excellence, 79, 80, 83, 90,
  92–93

Facets of Unity (Almaas), 7, 12, 16,
  18, 128
  cosmic consciousness in, 47
  holy ideas in, xxi, xxiii, 5,
    13, 153
  purpose of, xxi, xxiii
faith, 8, 51, 115–16
fear, 42, 48, 49, 52, 155–56
fearlessness, 32
feelings and sensations
  cessation of, 4
  detachment from, 148
  diamond guidance and,
    140–41
  incomplete understanding
    of, 53
  looking at, 119
  pleasure and, 112

Five (Ego-Stinge), 135–37
    idealized aspect, 137–39
    liberated, 143, 149
    soul child of, 159, 160
    See also diamond guidance
fixation
    age of setting, 158
    core and shell of, 5–6, 14–16
    ego ideal and, 18, 157
    of Eights, 25, 38
    Enneagon of, xv, xvi, xix
    Enneagram of, 2–3
    of Fours, 97, 101, 104
    freedom from, 7, 9, 21
    influences on, 61
    range of, 12
    recognizing, 126
    of Sevens, 107
    of Sixes, 44, 51, 54
    sleep in all, 123
    terms for, 11
    of Threes, 79, 80, 81, 92, 93
    unraveling, 21, 34
Four (Ego-Melan), 95–97
    idealized aspect, 97–98
    liberated, 104
    See also identity, essential
Fourth Way, xiii–xiv, xv, xviii, xix,
    xxii
Freud, Sigmund, 17, 68, 69, 143

Gabriel (angel), 141
generosity and giving, 55, 56, 62,
    66, 130, 132, 133, 134
Ginsburg, Ruth Bader, 137

gnosis, 30, 46–47, 99, 142, 145–46
God, 51, 130, 134, 160
Gödel, Kurt, 145
gold, merging, 100
    author's experience of, 85
    characteristics of, 61, 62–64
    disconnection from, 64–65
    integrating, 66
    as mother, 78
    presence of, 58–61
    in spiritual nature, 70
Great Work, 12, 76, 117
Greek philosophy, xi, 138
Gregory I, xvii
grief, 95, 102
groundedness, xix–xx, 20, 46,
    48–49, 51, 53, 125
Gurdjieff, George, xii–xiv, xv,
    xxii, 1, 2, 126, 155. *See also*
    Fourth Way

heart, 85, 109
    brilliancy in, 70
    distrusting, 114
    Markabah in, 113
    merging love and, 66
    mind and, 142
    opening, 36–37, 146, 155
    personal essence in, 88–89
    as presence, 60–61
    satisfaction of, 120
heart center, 45, 58, 146
heart point, 154
Helper. *See* Two (Ego-Flat)
Hepburn, Katharine, 95

spiritual practices
    distractions from, xvi
    heart opening as, 36–37
    necessity of, xii, 151
    "three days of prayer," 3
    true strength and, 34
Stalin, Joseph, 27, 32
steadfastness, 50, 51, 53, 54
strength, 70
    approximation/facsimile of,
        26–27, 31–32, 34
    of Eight, historical persons, 27
    essential, 30, 44, 127–28, 132,
        159 (see also strength, true)
    red, 29–30
    spiritual origin of, 30–31
    will and, 50
strength, true, 120
    access to, 38–39
    characteristics of, 27–28,
        31–34
    personality exploration
        approach, 35–38
    presence of, 27–30
    tantric approach, 34–35
stubbornness, 41, 48, 52–53
success, 79, 80–81, 83, 89,
        90–91, 92
suffering, 8
    compassion and, 146
    of Fours, 95, 105–6
    Nines' denial of, 125, 127
    Sevens' denial of, 108, 120
    welcoming, 146

Sufism, xi, xv, xx, 84, 91
    as Enneatype source, 1
    ideal in, 90
    Khidr in, 141
    states and stations in, 118
    true self in, 98
    See also lataif ("subtleties")
superego, 68, 69, 75, 77
surrender, 57, 60, 129, 156
sweetness, 58, 59, 66, 111, 119
synesthesia, 111–12
synthesis, 72, 78, 111–12, 139,
        143, 148, 149, 160

tantra, xx, 34–35, 52
Taoism, xv, 84, 85
Taylor, Elizabeth, 103
Tenzin Gyatso, Fourteenth Dalai
        Lama, 137, 139
"terror of the moment," 126
Thatcher, Margaret, 27
theory of holes, 21–22, 38, 39,
        152–53, 156
Three (Ego-Go), 79–81
    deficiency of, 22
    delusion, specific, 14, 15
    difficulty, specific, 13, 14, 15
    ego ideal, 16–17
    holy idea of, 14–15
    idealized aspect, 81–84
    liberated, 91
    quality, essential, 20
    reaction, specific, 13, 14
    See also personal essence

ABOUT THE AUTHOR

A. H. Almaas is the pen name of Hameed Ali, the Kuwaiti-born originator of the Diamond Approach, who has been guiding individuals and groups in Colorado, California, and Europe since 1976. Hameed was born in Kuwait in 1944. At the age of eighteen, he moved to the US to study at the University of California in Berkeley. Hameed was working on his PhD in physics when he reached a turning point in his life, and destiny led him to inquire into the psychological and spiritual aspects of human nature rather than the physical nature of the universe. He left the academic world to pursue an in-depth journey of inner discovery, applying his scientific precision and discipline to personal, experiential research. This included study with teachers in different modalities, extensive reading, and continuous study of his own consciousness in an effort to understand the essential nature of human experience and reality in general. Hameed's process of exploration led to the creation of the Ridhwan School and, with Karen Johnson, resulted in the founding and unfoldment of the Diamond Approach. He is the author of over nineteen different books, including *Love Unveiled*, *The Unfolding Now*, and *Runaway Realization*.

BOOKS BY A. H. ALMAAS

Essence with *The Elixir of Enlightenment*
Facets of Unity
The Inner Journey Home
Luminous Night's Journey
The Power of Divine Eros
Runaway Realization
Alchemy of Freedom
Keys to the Enneagram

Diamond Mind Series

Volume 1. The Void
Volume 2. The Pearl Beyond Price
Volume 3. The Point of Existence

Diamond Heart Series

Book One. Elements of the Real in Man
Book Two. The Freedom to Be
Book Three. Being and the Meaning of Life
Book Four. Indestructible Innocence
Book Five. Inexhaustible Mystery

Diamond Body Series

Spacecruiser Inquiry
Brilliancy
The Unfolding Now

The Journey of Spiritual Love Series

Love Unveiled